Dick Beauchamp
5/29/98

The Truth About Bichons

by Richard G. Beauchamp

Photograph by Missy.

The Truth About Bichons
Copyright 1998 by Richard G. Beauchamp

ISBN 0-9623515-1-2

Dedication
On rare occasions those of us who travel through the dog world are given an opportunity to experience true greatness. I was given that opportunity in my ownership of Ch. Chaminade Mr. Beau Monde. It is to his memory and his influence that this book is dedicated.

Acknowledgements
I wish to thank the many Bichon Frise fanciers who contributed to this work in both word and picture. Particular thanks are due the Bichon Frise Club of America, Inc. and the special Standard Committee that worked with me to produce the photos and diagrams that appear in *The Illustrated Discussion of the Bichon Frise* and from which excerpts are also reproduced here.

Published by The American Cocker Magazine. All rights reserved. No part of this book may be used or reproduced in any manner whatsoever, including electronic media or photocopying, without written permission from the publisher, except in the case of brief quotations embodied in critical reviews. For permission, write to Premiere Publications, Inc., 14531 Jefferson Street, Midway City, CA 92655-1030 USA, telephone (714) 893-0053, Fax (714) 893-5085.

Library of Congress Cataloging in Publication Data

This book is available at special quantity discounts for breeders and clubs for promotions, premiums, or educational use. Write for details.

Front Cover & page 1: Ch. Paw Mark's Fire and Ice, multiple Best in Show winner in America. Owned by Cecelia Ruggles, bred by Pauline Schultz and presented by Scott Sommer. Photograph by Missy.

Back Cover: Australian & New Zealand Ch. Shandau Fame Seeker, multiple Best in Show winner in Australia and New Zealand. Bred and owned by Elsie Rennie, Shandau Kennels, Auckland, New Zealand. Photograph by T. Dorizas.

Design and layout: Michael Allen

Printed in the United States of America

The Truth About Bichons
The Final Book in Richard Beauchamp's Bichon Frise Quartet

CONTENTS

5	About the Author
6	Preface
9	Chapter One *History*
47	Chapter Two *Transition of the Standards*
65	Chapter Three *Producing Patterns*
69	Chapter Four *Interpreting the Standard*
79	Chapter Five *Judging the Bichon Frise*
85	Chapter Six *Success in Breeding Bichons*
99	Chapter Seven *The Breeders Speak*
105	Chapter Eight *The International Breeder's Gallery*
150	Bibliography

Ch. Devon Puff and Stuff — *Photo by Ashbey*

About the Author

Richard G. ("Rick") Beauchamp was raised in the Midwestern part of the United States. His family kept field dogs—Irish and English Setters as well as Beagles. As a teenager, Rick chose American Cocker Spaniels to breed and exhibit himself.

Since then, he has been successfully involved in practically every facet of purebred dogs: breeding, exhibiting, professional handling, publishing, writing and judging. He has assisted in writing the official breed standards for several breeds and has lectured extensively throughout the world.

In the early 60s Rick moved to Hollywood, California where he served on the editorial staff of the entertainment industry "bible" *Daily Variety.* In 1964 Rick purchased *Kennel Review* magazine and developed it into one of the dog world's leading breeder—exhibitor magazines until publication was ceased upon his retirement in early 1992. It serves as the standard of excellence in its field to this day.

As a breeder-exhibitor he has been actively involved in breeds of nearly all the Variety Groups, including top winning Chow Chows, Dachshunds, Salukis and Irish Setters. His Beau Monde Kennel has produced quality Bichons Frises, Boxers, American Cocker Spaniels, Poodles, Wire Fox Terriers, Bull Terriers, Pembroke Welsh Corgis, Cavalier King Charles Spaniels and Chinese Shar-pei.

Bichons Frises have been his special area of interest since the early days of the breed. He was instrumental in achieving American Kennel Club recognition of the Bichon Frise and participated in writing the the AKC breed standard. Under the Beau Monde Kennel prefix he has bred nearly seventy AKC Bichon champions, many of them holding impressive Variety Group and Best In Show honors.

As a judge of all breeds with the Federacion Cynologique Internationale, he has judged championship events many times in Mexico, throughout the United Kingdom, Scandinavia, Europe, Australia, New Zealand, South Africa, the Orient, Central America and South America.

Rick is now judging in the United States for both the American Kennel Club and the United Kennel Club.

Preface

In 1969 I met my first Bichon Frise. Admittedly, I attended the meeting reluctantly, more as a matter of obligation than anything else. But as the fates would have it only a year later I owned my first Bichon Frise—a male puppy that I had, again reluctantly (I wanted a bitch) purchased from Barbara Stubbs. What is more, I had developed a more than passing fascination for this "new" old breed.

By 1971 my research had revealed that there was much more to this breed than what most American dog fanciers had assumed. If the average exhibitor here knew anything at all about the breed, the Bichon Frise was simply "that street dog from France."

I had found the breed had a much more intriguing story to tell. Its story had begun several centuries earlier and the breed had fallen in and out of favor on several different occasions and in many parts of the world.

Moreover, I realized that the general dog fancy's criticism of the breed ("there is no consistency of type") was due more to a lack of direction on the part of the neophyte American Bichon fanciers than it was to lack of defined characteristics. A very definitive standard had been written nearly four decades earlier in France.

In 1972, with the assistance of several notable breeders, I was able to write the first individual work ever to be published on the breed. The title of the small book was *The Bichon Frise Handbook*. The purpose of the book was to develop general awareness of the original 1933 French standard of the breed, address the questions surrounding trimming and grooming and to create some guidelines for those who were involved in breeding programs here in America.

It did not take us long to realize generalities were fine for breeds that had no impact on the all breed scene. However, the meteoric rise to success of the Bichon Frise demanded more details. We approached the problem in my second work on the breed, *The Bichon Frise Workbook*, published in 1975. At that time we began to address the breed standards ambiguous statement "body—slightly longer than tall." Those five words have undoubtedly been given more attention than all the others in the entire Bichon Frise Standard.

As breeders had more and more experience with the breed new discoveries were made and as is so often the case in doing research, each discovery led to yet another. New light was continually being shed upon what the breed was and should be. By the beginning of the 1980s the breed had already passed through the American Kennel Club's Miscellaneous class and had achieved full recognition as a member of the Non Sporting Group. Not only had the breed been accepted into the Non Sporting Group, it had become a formidable contender for group wins and even all breed Best In Show awards.

It was time to become even more definitive in what constituted a quality Bichon Frise. The Breed Standard Committee of the Bichon Frise Club of America began the painstaking task of making the existing standard more explicit. While their work continued in this area, expanded experience on the part of the many now involved with the breed led the way for me to write the third book in my Bichon series—*The Bichon Frise Today*.

This book reflected three things: First and foremost, there was an ever increasing desire on the part of the Bichon fancy in general for more detailed information in the area of breed type. It was obvious by then that the breed had arrived at a place at which we could be more demanding in defining what a quality specimen of the breed actually was, and last, but far from least, *The Bichon Frise Today* spoke directly to the judges who were given the responsibility of selecting the winners in our breed.

The 1980s and 1990s saw the breed grow from strength to strength around the world. A good part of this growth can be contributed to the two International Bichon Frise World Congresses. At these meetings topics of concern to all Bichon fanciers were discussed and this exchange of information assisted each country to both solve problems and make their own unique contributions to the breed.

Now, as we approach the new millennium there is need to see how what we have learned has actually benefited the breed. There is much to be learned by going directly to the experienced Bichon Frise breeders. We are able to tap their wealth of knowledge and make sure that it is not overlooked by future generations. Thus, this fourth and final installment in the Bichon Frise Quartet: *The Truth About Bichons*.

This book is not aimed at the novice. There have been many well written books devoted to health care and training—to the Bichon Frise in its roll as a companion. What is contained herein is directed toward the serious student of the breed, individuals who understand what has happened in the past to a breed is not easily swept under the rug. A breed's history determines what it is today and what must be dealt with in the future.

RICHARD G. BEAUCHAMP

Pictured below is Ch. Chamour Finale, the last champion for Mr. Beau Monde and #65, produced when he was 14 years of age.

Ch. Beau Monde Regal Rose

Photo by Ashbey

Chapter I
HISTORY OF THE BICHON FRISE

In order to truly understand the Bichon Frise it is important to know its origin and all the steps the breed has taken through the years to arrive at its appearance today. This helps answer the many questions a breeder will have in regard to why some characteristics can be eliminated or added in a single breeding while others vex a breeder for generations. The answers all lie in what occurred in the breed's journey from animal of the forest to ideal household companion.

All dogs, from the tiniest toy breed up to the most massive of the working breeds have one common ancestor - the wolf. The story of how the wolf evolved into man's best friend is as fascinating as it is old. It began well over ten thousand years ago in the dawning of history's Mesolithic period.

Among the wolf pack's habits there were a good number that may have struck a familiar note to early man. There was an obvious communal spirit and social order between members of the wolf pack and they employed these relationships in several ways including care of their offspring and in procuring food.

Man could well have been able to emulate some of the cooperative hunting techniques of the wolf pack while the wolf undoubtedly found an easily accessible food source in the food wastes man discarded outside the campsite. Thus, a symbiotic relationship could easily have established itself.

There is little doubt that the more amiable from the wolf packs were those apt to be granted access to man's campsites. In turn, the cubs of those more privileged wolves were born and raised in close proximity to humans, taking them one step further along the path to domestication.

It was found certain descendants of these steadily domesticated wolves were able to assist in a number of survival pursuits. An ability to bring down the fleet of foot game that roamed the land was of course particularly useful and earned the wolf an even more important place in the life of man.

Closer association was to reveal the wolf had an even wider variety of capabilities man could adapt to his own use. Soon these *wolves-cum-dogs* were performing a variety of duties: sounding the alarm when intruders approached, hauling heavy loads, going to earth after game and eventually, as man became increasingly more sophisticated, even assisting him in the retrieving of wounded game on both land and water. The wolf was evolving, slowly over many centuries, from *Canis Lupis*, the wolf, to *Canis Familiaris*, the dog.

One can find documentation of controlled breeding as early as the first century A.D. when the Romans had classified dogs into six general "groups": guard dogs, shepherd's dogs, hunting dogs (those hunting by sight and those hunting by scent), and fighting dogs.

Many breeds can be traced directly back to members of these early groups. Still other breeds were developed by combining individuals from two or more of these different categories to create yet another breed.

The combination we are primarily interested in is that which created the Bichon family. This new family was the result of combining the blood of a medium sized water spaniel type dog and a simultaneously existing family of light colored small "lap" or ladies' dogs that are said to have had their origin in the far East. The water spaniels were known a the Barbet. From this combination a small, often white, breed of dog evolved that was known as the "small Barbet" or Barbichon (later shortened simply to Bichon). The combination that produced the Barbichon also proved to be the basis for a number of other small "companion" breeds, not the least of which were the Poodle and the Maltese.

As man developed a more sophisticated life-style and urbanization occurred, smaller dogs became very popular. Instead of being the sole domain of the male hunting members of the family, the smaller dogs moved indoors and became members of the immediate household, women and children included.

Because they were small enough, these companion dogs often traveled with their owners, many of which were seamen. These rough and ready men took the little dogs along as reminders of the homes they would not see for many months at a time.

The little Bichons that had eventually evolved crossed the seas along the trade routes of the world and were often left behind in trade for other goods. The dogs became established and flourished in their new homes, developing into distinct varieties.

These became known as the Bichon Maltaise, the Bichon Bolognaise, the Bichon Havanese and the Bichon Teneriffe. It is the Bichon Teneriffe that is chiefly credited as the forerunner of today's Bichon Frise. However, as we will see, the similar origin of all bichons, their subsequent inter-related historics and their physical similarities make crediting the dog from Teneriffe as the Bichon Frise's only ancestor a dubious distinction. Problems of type plaguing the Bichon Frise to this day constantly recall what might be considered distinctive characteristics of their close relatives.

The Four Bichon Varieties

It is also important to keep in mind that no one really knows what happened to the little dogs during their stays in the many foreign ports of the world. Nor are we certain of what their gene pools carried back to Europe upon their return journeys generations later. There is, however, ample agreement to substantiate where the dogs went and it is more than certain that the first of the group, the Bichon Maltaise, flourished on the isle of Malta.

Whether this breed is the ancestor of today's Maltese remains controversial. Those who believe this to be so cite as proof the recurring incorrect woolly coat that some Maltese have to this day. The standard of the Maltese requires a coat that is straight and silky with no undercoat whatsoever

The Bolognaise became very popular in and around the Italian city of Bologna. The dogs were often seen in the company of members of the royal family and their court. Because they were favorites of the Italian royalty they became prestigious gifts for members of the French and Spanish courts as well.

There is not a great deal of discernible difference between today's Bichon Bolognaise and the Bichon Frise (nee Teneriffe). The temperament of the Bolognaise is said to be less extroverted than that of its cousin and the Bolognaise is found to be proportionately higher on leg and shorter in body that the Bichon Frise. Then too, the Bolognaise is presented in the show ring with scissoring done only around the eyes and feet.

Other migrations of the little companion dogs took them through the Mediterranean to Spain and traveling with the Spanish sailors the little dogs found a new home in Cuba. These are credited as being the forebears of the variety known as the Bichon

Havanese. The Havanese is the smallest member of the bichon family—normally about 8 to 11 inches at the shoulder. The Havanese is shorter on leg, longer in body, and has a much finer coat. A wide variety of colors is allowed in the breed and the colors can be both solid and broken.

It is worth noting that the original French standard of the Bichon Frise breed included a clause that made "black spots in the coat" a disqualification. Though all but unheard of in the breed today, one can only surmise it represented a problem at one stage of the breed and could easily have been a result of Havanese influence.

No doubt these same Spanish sailors took other members of the bichon family with them in their trading expeditions to the Canary Islands and Teneriffe as well. It can only be assumed the indigenous breeds of these islands crossed with the bichon type dogs left behind by the Spaniards. But flourish they did and generations later their descendants made their way full circle not only back to Spain but to Italy as well. This variety of bichon was known then as the Bichon Teneriffe and the breed was to carry that name for many years.

France Renames the Dog from Teneriffe

A good deal of controversy surrounds the when and where of the name "Bichon Frise," but we do know that *The Encyclopedia of Dogs (Thomas Y. Crowell Co., New York)* produced under direction of The Federation Cynologique Internationale (FCI) gives the Bichon Frise's country of origin as France. The FCI is the organization that has given itself the responsibility of deciding upon all things canine throughout Europe.

During the 1500s the French were highly influenced by Italy's Renaissance and it was very fashionable in France to adopt everything Italian. Part of the fashion trend in the French Courts was Italy's little white Bichon Teneriffe. Francis I, patron of the Renaissance (1515—1547 A.D.), was particularly fond of the breed during his reign.

Little appears in French literature about the Teneriffe dog after that period until the rise of Napoleon III into power in the early years of the nineteenth century. The Bichon Teneriffe is frequently mentioned in French literature during that century and is frequently portrayed with members of the royal courts in the works of leading artists of the period.

By the end of the nineteenth century the breed was to be replaced in the favor of the court but hardy breed that it was the Bichon Teneriffe survived and would more often than not be found in the streets of Paris

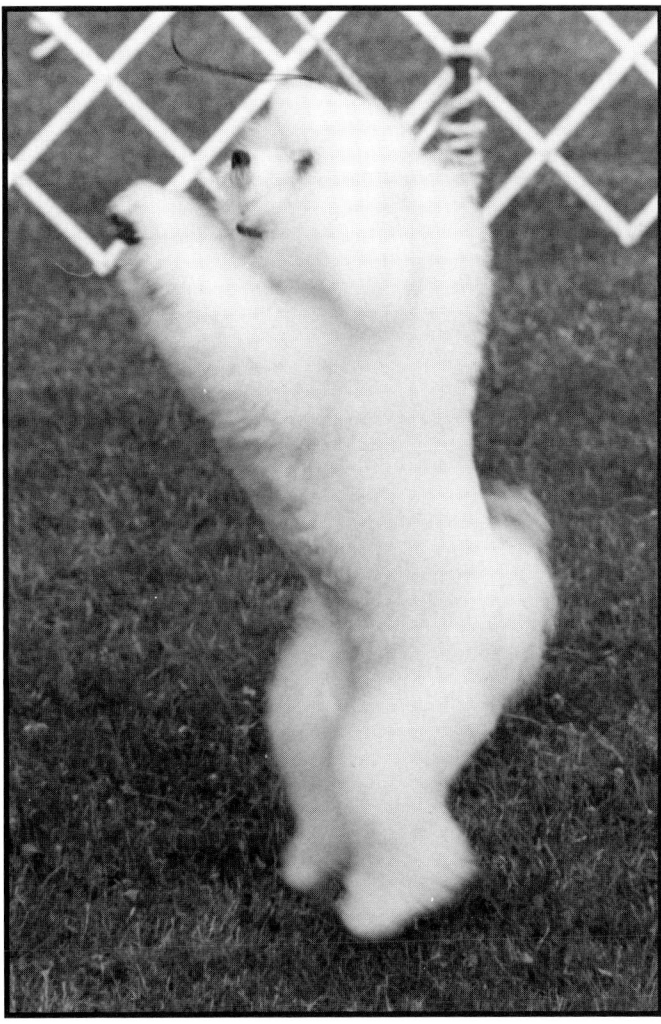

Ch. Devon's Puff and Stuff takes a break at a show and demonstrates the charm of the breed.

and other cities accompanying tradesmen and street musicians. The nimble Bichons were highly trainable and loved to perform for the crowds. The breed demonstrated a unique ability to walk on its hind legs for long distances and usually did so while pawing the air which passersby interpreted as begging for money and the people good humoredly responded.

Europe's great circuses and carnivals took advantage of the Bichon's extroverted personalities and uncanny ability to learn and perform tricks. The dogs were undoubtedly bred and the offspring selected with the ability to entertain foremost in mind. To this day the breed retains its entertaining capabilities and Bichon owners are amazed to find their dogs walking on their hind legs, performing somersaults and performing feats of dexterity with no training what-so-ever.

Were it not for the indestructible constitution of the Bichon, however, the breed could well have been lost to us during the First and Second World Wars. Reduced to minimal numbers by the end of World War I the breed escaped extinction only through the efforts of a few valiant fanciers who gathered what remained of the breed from the streets of France and Belgium. Working cooperatively those who found pleasure in the happy little dogs were able to obtain breed recognition under the auspices of the Societe Centrale Canine in March of 1933. The breed was officially given the name "the Bichon A Poil Frise" which, translated into English, is "the Bichon of the curly hair."

Just when it looked as though devotees had secured the future of the Bichon Frise, another great war threatened the newly named breed. Here again the breed's hardiness and the determination of its owners assisted the Bichon Frise through this next devastating ordeal.

There can be little doubt that the checkered history of the Bichon Frise through the centuries included liaisons with its three cousins and even though the breed was classified, legitimized if you will, by the French in 1933 what remained of the breed in Europe after the close of World War II could only have been a conglomerate of the bichon varieties.

This, combined with the practice in some European countries of permitting dogs of unknown parentage to be registered and used as breeding stock saved the Bichon Frise from total extinction. On the other hand it would prove to severely complicate the task of setting type.

That the practice of accepting dogs of unknown parentage into some European stud books continued on until as late as 1969 is evidenced by a letter written on May 31 of that year by Albert Baras, then president of the Club Belge du Bichon. He wrote in answer to a letter of inquiry from the Bichon Frise Club of America as follows:

". . . Excuse me for this very late answer but we were too busy with our International Exhibitions in Bussel (sic). At this exhibition my wife received first honor price (sic) with our PUCE (a female new blood).

We say new blood when the dog comes from an unknown origin . . . or when the parents or the grandparents come from unknown origin . . . but has been presented and examinated (sic) by three different judges? Usually those bichon (sic) are really more beautiful coming from usual lines (too much consanguinity - too much inbreeding as you say)!!!

This is in no way meant to condemn European breeders for their actions. Were it not for their resourcefulness many breeds would have become entirely extinct during the war years. The Bichon Frise was certainly no exception.

Mr. Barases' reference to inbreeding may well have been an understatement on his part. It is interesting to examine the breeding program of one kennel that was to have significant bearing on bloodlines later coming to the U.S.

The Milton Line

In the 1930s Mon. and Mme. A. Bellotte of Brussels embarked upon a breeding program under their Milton suffix which was to have a far greater influence on the breed throughout the world than I'm sure the couple could ever have anticipated. The line began with a dog, Pitou, whelped in approximately 1929 and a bitch, Dora of Milton, whelped sometime in 1930. Pitou produced Bambin of Milton out of the bitch Ch. Bomba of Milton. Bambin in turn was bred to Quinette of Milton. Quinette was by Ch. Pitou of Milton (another Pitou son) out of Dora of Milton. This mating produced Ch. Ufolette of Milton.

Bambin was subsequently bred to Ufolette producing a son, Ch. Youbi of Milton. Youbi was bred back to his dam, Ufolette, producing Gisette of Milton. This was in the 1950s. The already intently inbred Giselle began as intense an inbred line as one could witness. She was bred to her brothers, sons, grandsons, and they in turn inbred to their littermates, sons, daughters and grandchildren. Is it any wonder that the faults and virtues stemming from Milton continue to exist?

Kennel names with which American breeders are familiar descending from the Milton line are: Villa-Sainval (Belgium), Chaponay (Belgium), and de la Buthrie (France-combined with Steren Vor).

In France the Steren Vor line of Mme. Adabie was also to have far reaching influence, not only in Europe but later in America as well. No less inclined to inbreeding, the line eventually influenced several kennel names figuring significantly in American pedigrees.

Steren Vor stands significantly behind familiar American foundation stock names such as de Bourbriel, d'Egriselles, Frimousettes, Wanarbry and von Goldfischbrunner.

Carlise Cicero of Tresilva had 12 first prizes, a reserve BIS, 2 Best Puppy in Show, a Best Rare Breed and a Best of Breed, all while still under 11 months.

In summarizing this chapter, the reader should take note of the diverse background of the breed. The four varieties of Buchon: Maltese, Havanese, Bolognaise and Teneriffe (or Bichon Frise) all had distinct influences upon each other.

It appears the differences separating the Varieties were not eliminated by the incredible inbreeding programs of the European breeders - only perpetuated. The first few Bichons that were to cross the ocean to America carried every fault and every virtue of their diverse ancestry.

The Bichon Comes to America

1952 was an important year for the Bichon Frise in that Helene and Francois Picault of Deippe, France became interested in the breed. In a letter to Mrs. Azalea Gascoigne that was later published in the newly formed Bichon Frise Club of America bulletin, the Picaults were to write in part:

"Dear Mrs. Gascoigne: As you have asked us so politely I am going to relate to you how we became breeders. In 1952 my wife was a frequent visitor at the home of a friend who had a little Bichon Frise, and she became filled with enthusiasm over the adorable little ways and manners of this pretty Bichon. I promised myself that on my wife's next birthday I would give her a pretty little Bichon Frise. And in 1952 my wife had her first Bichon named Michou. My wife and I adored animals. (This, moreover, is indeed the first requirement in a breeder.) Michou was a pampered child even having his own little bed. Then we had to have a little female to make a little breeding family. It was then that we became acquainted with Mme. Abadie, President of the Bichon Club in France, who sold us Etoile de Steren Vor, a darling little two month old dog. And five months later, in July of 1955, we decided to participate in the dog show at Dieppe, the city where we lived and where we were engaged in business as wholesale confectioners. We were next to Mme. Abadie (neighbors) at the show. She was showing her international champion, Hors Concours Bandit de Steren Vor and a young dog, Cannard Blue who had already won many first prizes and which she wanted to campaign to its championship because Bandit was getting old.

We conversed together and she told us that she had been to see her daughter in New York with a little Bichon. And that a man had told her 'Bit (sic) Madame, if you would breed these pretty little dogs here you would make a small fortune! We asked her when she planned to leave. She answered that in view of her age she did not forsee such an eventuality. We told her, then, that it would be us who would go to make that little fortune in America as we thought of leaving constantly to rejoin our two daughters married to Americans. That day Michou had a 2nd prize and Etoile a first prize. But Mme. Abadie made us understand that Michou, not having an official pedigree could not be bred to Etoile without risk of ruining the line. We decided, then that day, to get a pretty little male to create our breeding program. The male arrived several months later and was called Eddie White de Steren Vor. Our breeding was established and wisely we made the acquaintance of the Kennel Club. Having completed all the formalities several months later we got our breeder's license under the name "Elevage de Hoope." From May to August 1956 Etoile de Steren Vor and her little future husband, Eddie White de Steren Vor competed in different shows in Normandy, Ruen, Le Havre, Deauville, Dieppe... 17 first prizes. And the 19th of October we took the boat from Havre (our final destination being Milwaukee) accompanied by our three darlings, the three we had acquired from Mme. Abadie previously, four little females to complete our breeding. Two dogs would come to us by air in 1957. They were Gavote and Gypsie de Wamarby. They arrived at the time of Etoile's first litter, 5 pups. This gave us a total of 10 dogs. We wanted to present our dogs at the first Milwaukee show (after our arrival). But a great disappointment awaited us. Our entries were refused because our dogs were not recognized by AKC. Having the true spirit of the breeder we decided to take our dogs and parade in front of the entrance to the dog show with our 10 babies. There were five of us and each had two dogs on leash. But this wasn't enough! We decided to enter the hall. Our puppies were adorable and we placed a tri-color cockade on each collar. It made a pretty effect. And it gained the admiration of spectators who coming in to the show. About a half hour after our arrival (in the hall) a furious man appeared who told us to get out immediately and if we didn't he would call the police. We left then, furious but happy at the same time, for having made our demonstration. We had the publicity and one day we were invited to present our dogs in show . . . the exposition at Green Bay. And it was there that we met Mme. Gascoigne, a breeder from Pewaukke. This lady was enchanted with the beauty and sweetness of these little animals.

My wife had 17 dogs in our apartment and it was remarkable that she take (sic) care of them all in perfect condition. Then in 1960 our children decided to leave Milwaukee for California and proposed that we accompany them and I vow to you it was without regret that we left Milwaukee (7 months of cold!) for the country of the sun.

We left then with 13 dogs, they were sent by rail leaving two days before us and arrived the same day we did, or seven days after their departure. But there a great disappointment awaited us. Our children had bought a motel in Coronado but it did not have a place for our babies. We decided to put them in a boarding kennel at a veterinarian who charged us $200 a month

and we were not allowed to make contact with them. Needless to say, deprived of our little animals we were very unhappy, and each evening my wife and I would prowl around the kennel to try to catch sight of our babies. This martyrdom for us, and for our animals also, lasted two months.

As is usually the case in dogs, the anticipated "fortune" never was to come for the Picaults. The family of Bichons grew rapidly while sales for animals not registered with the AKC were hard to come by regardless of the breed's charm. During 1960 and 1961 a few breeders acquired stock from the Picaults and a few others imported stock from France and Belguim.

A Fortuitious Meeting

In 1961 the Picaults were at the end of their patience and finances when, as fate would have it, they met Gertrude Fournier of San Diego who, enchanted with the breed, felt sure she could assist them in securing publicity and eventual recognition for the white charmers.

Mrs. Fournier had gained some note as a Collie breeder under the Cali-Col prefix but to signify the establishment of a new partnership with the Picaults the name Pic-Four was coined honoring the surnames of both interested parties.

Still, however, fame and recognition continued to elude the breed and the Picaults were again denied their dreamed-of fortune. The limits of the partnership were to create discontent for both parties and through a series of events Mrs. Fournier became sole owner of the previously mentioned Eddy White de Steren Vor, Etoille de Steren Vor, Gipsie de Wanarbry and Gigi de Hoop.

Later when it became apparent that an outcross was needed Mrs. Fournier imported the intensely inbred sisters Lyne and Lassy of Milton from Belguim. Marquis of Milton was a later import. While her purebred dog associates considered Mrs. Fournier's breed "cute" and blessed wilh an obvious charm, their bedraggled appearance and lack of style held little appeal to American fanciers. Still she persevered. Had she not, there is every reason to believe the breeds rise to world-wide fame would never have taken place.

It was at about this same time that Mrs. Fournier, who had reverted back to her prior kennel name Cali-Col, acquired a list of buyers who had obtained puppies from the Picaults during their stay in Milwaukee. From the list it was determined that all the males had been sold as pets. One name, however, stood out as being a breeder of note in Dachshunds. This was Azalea Gascoigne of Azavic Kennels.

By advertising in purebred dog publications they were able to arouse the interest of two more Bichon fanciers actively involved in other breeds. One, Jean Rank, was from the east coast; the other, Goldie Olson, was from Oregon.

First Annual Meeting

When Azalea Gascoigne was contacted it was discovered that she had formed the Bichon Frise Club of America (BFCA), in Milwaukee. Its membership consisted of those who had purchased the previously mentioned pet stock. The club was soon to be reorganized, naming Mrs. Gascoigne as the first president and Gerturde Fournier was named Secretary and Registrar in 1964. For this purpose Mrs. Gascoigne visited San Diegö to become better acquainted with other fanciers and to formulate the constituion and By-Laws of the new parent club. Mrs. Olson also came from Oregon and with the local B.F.C.A. membership including a new California breeder, Mayree Butler, the first annual meeting was held and breed standard accepted. There was a charter membership of 28 Bichon owners.

Mrs. Gascoigne was accompanied by a young male Bichon she had bred herself. His sire was Andre de Gascoigne of the Picault's breeding and his dam was a bitch Mrs. Gascoigne had purchased herself on a trip to France, Lady des Frimousetts. The dogs name was Dapper Dan de Gascoigne.

Mrs. Gascoigne left Dapper Dan behind when she returned to Milwaukee and he, along with the stock already present in San Diego, was to set the pattern for the American Bichon; an animal which was not only to recapture the interest of the entire dog world but to become one of the world's most formidable show competitors.

By 1966 club membership had grown to 90 and more than 300 dogs were registered with BFCA. Within 4 years membership totaled 400 representing 38 states, Canada, Alaska, and Hawaii. Individual registrations had risen to 1,040 dogs and a new standard had been written.

Impeccable records were kept by the new registrar Mayree Butler and it is without doubt her flawless stud book was to play a strong part in the breed's painless transfer to the A.K.C. registration system.

Barbara Stubbs was a resident of nearby La Jolla, California and she, along with her daughter Wendy had been intensely involved in horses. Barbara's son Bruce meanwhile had developed an interest in purebred dogs. To support his interest mother and son soon discovered the Bichon Frise and became owners of two dogs, Petit Galant de St. George and Cali-Col's Robspierre and a bitch Reenroy's Ami du Kilkanney. This was to prove another incredible stroke of good fortune for

Photo by Missy

the breed. What the breed was lacking at this point was style. The ungroomed Bichon held little interest for glamour minded American dog fanciers. And, in addition to its own lack of style it had no members of the "upper echelons" of the dog world to assist its cause. It appeared to Mrs. Stubbs that there were two routes that could be followed: (1) a broad based exposure of the breed to the general public hoping that this in turn would create interest on the part of active breeders and exhibitors. Or, (2) another alternative was to aim for the top, involving well known A.K.C. judges, handlers, and fanciers in the breed right from the beginning. She chose the latter course and with her decision to persue this course, the breed began to "cook on all four burners," as the saying goes.

The First Haircut

Mrs. Stubbs, through their mutual involvement in horses, was able to secure the services of the then noted dog handler Frank T. Sabella as guest speaker at the 1969 Annual Match and meeting. He was asked to give a grooming demonstration and advise the club members in regard to presentation of the Bichon.

Mr. Sabella spent the night prior to the annual meeting at the La Jolla home of his close friends Major and Beatrice Godsol, internationally renowned all breed judges. The three "talked dogs" into the wee hours of the morning and although he had a world wide reputation as a groomer par excellence, Sabella admitted to the Godsols that he hadn't the vaguest notion as to what to suggest to the Bichon Fanciers regarding presentation of their breed the following day.

Mr. Godsol was adamant that the breed would never achieve AKC recognition and it mattered little how they were trimmed. Mrs. Godsol, on the other hand, admitted to having observed the dogs at matches in a nearby La Jolla park and that while the entries were made up of dogs of many dissimilar types there was something unique and special that they all possessed. "It has something to do with the way their little faces are framed in that white halo of hair. Those shoe button eyes and nose just seem to punctuate that impish look they have," Mrs. Godsol said. Her words gave Sabella the much needed inspiration he sought for his demonstration the next day. At this momentous event he called for grooming that would accentuate and frame the lively, animated expression of the Bichon. His attention, like the previous night's converstation, was centered primarily on the head. The rest of the dog was summarily dismissed with "clean, white, well brushed dog with a natural look". Even at that it convinced the "doubting Thomases" that the breed was not about to make it on the Amercian scene with out proper bathing and brushing.

The Kennel Review Years

At this point Mrs. Stubbs began a scries of phone calls to *Kennel Review* magazine doing her utmost to ignite a spark of interest for her cause. All I knew

Bruce Stubbs with Rip (litter brother to the breed's first BIS winner, Ch. Chaminade Syncopation) in the early 1970s. Photo by Missy.

about the Bichon Frise at this point was what I had heard from others: "Giant Maltese I think—something like that." It didn't sound at all appealing. By phone Mrs. Stubbs extended a personal invitation to have me attend the annual meeting and match to be held January 24, 1970 at the Charter House Hotel in Anaheim. Thelma Brown was to judge, ""Perhaps *Kennel Review* could give the show some coverage," she suggested. Still, there was practically no interest on my part. However, to cut the converstation short I did promise coverage of the event—if not by myself at least by a staff member. There was no doubt in my mind at the time as to who would *not* do the covering!

The introductory coverage appeared in the December 1970 Annual edition of *Kennel Review*, creating at least a little interest on the part of the Amcrican dog fancy. Actually, the photographs submitted portrayed a beast with greater appeal then what I had suspected. But, our duty had been executed and the matter was closed. *I thought!* Not so. Mrs. Stubbs had other plans! The plans included (a) a visit by her to the *Kennel Review* offices and (b) my personally viewing the dogs.

She arrived with her trio in tow—Petit Galant (Henry), Robspierre (Ben) and Ami. They were done out to a fare-thee-well. Groomed, bathed chalked and ready to walk in and win Westminster. The little white charmers dazzled me with their jaunty attitude and beguilling faces and quite frankly Barbara Stubbs herself was a knockout! Three white dogs and the lady in black! I was hooked!

Ch. Chaminade Mr. Beau Monde with his first two champions, Beau Monde The Author (top) and Beau Monde The Actor (bottom). Photo by Missy.

Through the following Spring and Summer Mrs., Stubbs and I spoke by phone frequently, outlining plans for attaining AKC recognition while discussing tried-and-true breeding combinations and approaches. During the course of these conversations she mentioned a highly anticipated litter sired by Cali-Col's Robspierre out of Reenroy's Ami du Kilkanny that was due in August of 1970.

Due to other committments I was unable to attend any of the matches or functions the Bichon club held. However, on October 25, 1970 a friend, Tom Roh, and I attended the Associated Rare Breeds Club Match held in Fontana, Californnia. Mrs. Harriet Taylor judged and there were 29 Bichons entered.

In the classes were names which were later to become historically significant: Seascape The Captain's Choice, Ee's-R Royale Trinquette, Chaminades' Phoenicia, and Mel-Mar's Imperial du Chaminade. Other important individuals shown were: Cali-Col's Robspierre, Cali-Col's Shadrack, and Ee's-R Cali-Col Ritzy Ruffles. Several youngsters from the previously referred to Ami litter were entered as well—two males, Chaminade's Fortissimo and Chaminades Capriccio; and a bitch Chaminade Sonata.

I handled Sonata at this, her first show. She was just 10 weeks old and together we won the 2-4 months Puppy Bitch class. It was the first time I had seen as many Bichons together as were entered that day and while it was immediately apparent there was an incredibly vast array of types being bred, some order began to develop for me.

Scanning the entire lot a singular type and expression began to emerge—more in some, less in others, but it did exist in them all. It was then I realized just how much the bitch, Ami du Kilkanny, expressed this breed character—its "essence" if you will. If the breed was ever going to make it on the American dog scene, it would have to be of the type and style she represented, I was sure. She satisfied the dog man's need for line, proportion and balance, combining it with a remarkable elegance and distinct type. It was then and there I decided to get back into dogs again on a personal basis. Because of my position as publisher of *Kennel Review* I had ceased breeding and showing all the previous breeds I had owned. However, now I was intrigued and challenged,and furthermore this breed offered no competition to our advertising Non-Sporting Group clients. Additionally, helping to get the breed recognized would indeed be a project to keep me occupied for a good long time to come.

I wanted a bitch and it had to be an Ami daughter. That was that! Fate decreed otherwise. Marvel Brown had already spoken for Chaminade Sonata, the only bitch in Ami's litter. The choice male of the three, then called Chaminade Capriccio,was available however.

Capriccio was more his mother's type than any of the others in the litter and since I really didn't want to raise puppies anyway, a male would have to do. I decided to take "Christopher" as he was called and Mrs. Stubbs and I agreed that he would be registered as Chaminade Mr. Beau Monde. He came to live with me as an "apartment dog" in November, 1970.

The following months found me reading, research-

ing and studying everything I could get my hands on. At the same time the fancy-at-large began to take note of the fuzzy white dogs that appeared with ever increasing regularity in *Kennel Review*. In my frequent travels throughout the country I answered question after question regarding the nature of the Bichon and their potential as candidate for AKC recognition. I could highly recommend them as companions and "yes" I was very optimistic about their future with the AKC.

The editorial support the breed earned in *Kennel Review* was the type of publicity Barbara Stubbs had sought and exactly what the breed needed. America was paying *a lot* of attention!

The Bichon Frise Club of America was far from idle at this point either. Their annual Specialty matches drew outstanding entries and attendance as they moved about the country. Above all, the club had the foresight to employ the services of notable and knowledgeable figures to judge these matches. Among them were the aforementioned Thelma Brown, Anna K. Nicholas, Haworth Hoch, Clark Thomson, David Doane, Ann Rogers Clark, Dr. Samuel Draper, Ann Stevenson, and Irene Schlintz. Not a shabby list for any breed, especially for one not even recognized by the AKC!

In September 1971 the A.K.C. accepted the Bichon Frise into Miscellaneous Class competition. Within months the breed literally dominated the Miscellaneous Classes and the domination culminated at the International Kennel Club of Chicago in April 1972. On that date Chaminade Mr. Beau Monde won the largest single class of Miscellaneous Dogs in AKC history to that point. There were 38 males alone of all Miscellaneous breeds shown and the judge was Edd Embry Bivin. Mr. Beau Monde was shown to the win by Joe Waterman.

Local breed clubs were springing up in all parts of the country. Interest on the part of breeders in other breeds accelerated rapidly. Things could not have gone more smoothly.

A Look at the Standard

In 1972, with the assistance of several breeders I wrote the first known individual work to be published on the breed, *The Bichon Frise Handbook*. It included an interpretation of the standard then in effect. It was

Ch. Beau Monde Drewlane Demon and a 7 week old puppy bitch

the first attempt made to correlate type and soundness and the first time the breed's actual proportions were set down concretely to serve as a guideline for breeders and judges. These proportions were gleaned from the original French breed standard written in 1933. It was at this time that I first began to really appreciate the qualities of type and soundness the Mr. Beau Monde dog had. He was the embodiment of that first French Standard—fitting it like a glove.

Of equal significance in the little Handbook was the section on trimming by Frank Sabella. Experimental trimming by many of the breeders, observations of the various styles being used and conversations with Mr. Sabella led us to several conclusions.

First, it was monumentally important to maintain the powder puff look the original French Standard called for. Secondly, there had to be form and style to the trim or the breed would simply never catch on in America.

It had been years since I had groomed dogs—not since my days in Cockers. The more I thought about the Cocker though the more I realized how attractive and serviceable the 9 or 10 month old Cocker puppy looked in respect to the body and cylindrical leg grooming. The length of coat achieved by the young Cocker at this stage of development was attractive (yes, even powder puff looking!) and at the same time permitted the observer to see what the animals four legs were doing when it moved. That look could be most readily adapted to the Bichon.

Now we had a workable and attractive body and leg trim to accompany the Godsol-Sabella inspired head trim which had by this time been incorporated into the exhibitors grooming techniques everywhere.

In two years time the breed had attracted so much attention and such universal acceptance by dog fanciers it was hard to believe that it was not in fact a fully accredited AKC breed.

Full Recognition

And then late in 1972 it was announced that two Miscellaneous Class breeds had been granted full recognition by the A.K.C. and would be eligible for point competition on April 8, 1973. The breeds were the Akita, which had spent nearly 20 years in Miscellaneous and the Bichon Frise which had spent just past a year in that class! An astounding and record setting length of time. Yet another first for the Bichon!

Fittingly enough, the Bichon Frise Club of San Diego was host for the Specialty Match held the day prior to the breed's debut into point competition. The judge was Tom Stevenson and there were 53 puppies and 58 adults entered for a combined entry of 111

Australian Ch. Nagazumi Mr. Frosty of Zudik (imp. UK), Best of Breed at the Melbourne Royal Show in 1984. Photo by Robinson.

actual dogs. Again the Bichon set the dog fancy on its ear! Handling dogs at this show—all competing for Best in Match (no points mind you) were no less than 13 professional handlers. Not just handlers, but *"handlers"!* A match show with the likes of Jane Forsyth, Peggy Hogg, Frank Sabella, Ted Young, Jr. and Joe Waterman handling! But that's not all, also in the ring that day were Richard Bauer, Jeffrey Lynn Brucker, Barbara Humphries, Ric Byrd, Ric Chashoudian, Mike Dougherty, Fran Wasserman, and Betty Jeanne Orseno. You didn't need a crystal ball to know that this breed's future was secure. It was already firmly ensconced as a dues paying member of the American dog scene. The winners that day were: Best Adult—Gertrude Fournier's Cali-Col's Scalawag; Best Opposite—Bruce Stubbs' Reenroy's Ami du Kilkanny; Best Puppy—Mildred Sharitze's Cali-Col's Vanguard.

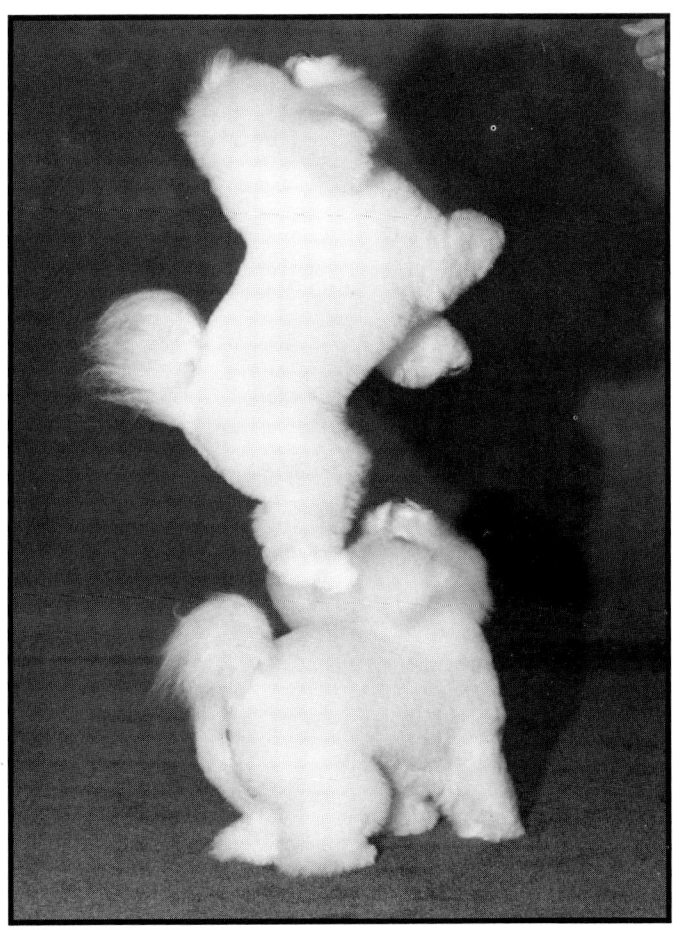

Photo by Ashbey

The following day Mrs. Winifred Heckmann judged the breed's first point show at Silver State Kennel Club. Her selection for Winners Dog, Best of Winners and Best of Breed was Gertrude Fournier's Cali-Col's Scalawag (Dapper Dan de Gascoigne ex Cali-Col's Our Daphne); Winner Bitch, Best Opposite Sex was Tenna Sarkissian's Chaminade Phoenicia (Petit Galant de St. George ex Reenroy's Cest Bon Pigalle). Scalawag then went on to place second in the Non Sporting Group under Mr. John Cramer.

The History Makers

The first Bichon Frise to complete its American Championship was Charles and Dolores Wolskie's C & D Count Kristopher who was sired by Peppe de Barnette and out of Quentia of Goldysdale.

The first all breed Best In Show to be won by a Bichon was Framington Valley Kennel Club on July 7, 1973. Mrs. William Tabler's Ch. Chaminade Syncopation (Petit Galant de St. George ex Ch. Chaminade Sonata) was selected for the award by Mr. Louis Murr, just three short months after the breed had gained AKC recognition. The handler was Ted Young, Jr.

George Ann Slocum's Ch. C and D's Beau Monde Sunbeam (Ch. Chaminade Mr. Beau Monde ex Ch. C and D's Countess Becky) was the breed's first Best In Show bitch. She topped the Longview Kennel Club entry on March 20, 1974 under Winifred Heckmann. The handler was Joe Waterman.

The first Bichon to win Best of Breed at Westminster was Robert Koeppel's Ch. Rank's Eddie (Martin's Frostie Muffin ex Rank's Treasure). The award was made by Melboume T. L. Downing, the handler was Richard Bauer and the date was February, 1974.

Wendy Kellerman became the first Junior Showman ever to win her class division with a Bichon Frise at Westminster K.C. on February 10, 1977. She handled her own Ch. Beau Monde Works D'Arte Witty

Photo by Missy

(Reenroy's Sir Barnard ex Works D'Arte Renoir) to the historic win.

The first Best In Show at a National Specialty was won by Nan and Burt Busk's Ch. Vogelflight's Music Man (Ch. Chaminade Mr. Beau Monde ex Ch. Vogelflight's Diandee Amy Pouf). He was handled by Pauline Waterman and the judge was Langdon Skarda.

The first bitch to win Best In Show at the National Specialty was Nancy Shapland's Crockerly Beau Monde Eclipse (Ch. Beau Monde The Huckster ex Ch. C and D's Beau Monde Moonshine). She was handled to the win by Joe Waterman in May, 1980 under judge Dr. Samuel Draper.

To the casual observer the Bichon's success had been meteoric but fourteen years had elapsed since Gertrude Fournier's first meeting with Helene and Francois Picault in San Diego. Mrs. Fournier's faith, determination and dedication were unswerving. Where most would have conceded to the apparently insurmountable obstacles, she perservered. Though the efforts of many assisted the breed along its way, they would have not had the opportunity to do so had it not been for Mrs. Fournier's faith in the charming white dogs from France.

Defining Proportions

The early success of the Bichon Frise on the all breed level in the U.S. left little doubt in the minds of fanciers that the breed's future as a showdog was secure. However, it also became apparent as the 1970s wore on that questions demanding answers were being asked by individuals outside of the breed.

What once were matters of more or less unspoken agreement among fanciers themselves, were no longer satisfactory. It was obvious that a clarification of the standard with which the breed had gained AKC acceptance was needed.

What had given breeders general guidance in the early years was proving not nearly specific enough for judges who were required to make fine line decisions. Neither was the standard specific enough to provide answers for new breeders who were trying to create more consistency in what they were producing.

Confusion Reigns

The most frequent questions arose in regard to proportions; specifically what was right in regard to the breed's height to body length ratio. The first standard of the breed that had been adopted by the original 28 members of the BFCA was amended in 1968 and stated only, "Body—Slightly longer than tall." Obviously the word "slightly" meant something different to each person reading it—an inch to one person and just as easily 4 inches to someone else.

We also realized there was a great deal of confusion as to what specifically was being referred to when the term "body" was used. Some interpreted this to mean the distance from sternum to buttocks was what should be longer than the dog was tall. Others took the statement to mean the distance from highest point of the shoulder (withers) to tail was what was being referred to. Obviously these two approaches resulted in dogs of vastly different proportions. One created a dog that was off square, the other a dog that was substantially longer in body.

Using the first approach, in which the distance from sternum to buttocks is considered "body," and is what should be slightly longer than the dog's height, the back (withers to tailset) would then, by necessity, be slightly shorter than the dog's height measurement.

If the distance from withers to tailset were to be considered "body" (and is what should be longer than tall) it is obvious this would be a dog whose measurement from sternum to buttocks would be *considerably* longer than the dog's height measurement.

To help add fuel to the fire of controversy, the original imports into the U.S. ran the entire proportion gamut. (Certainly not surprising with the indiscriminate history of the breed). In truth, however, some of these dogs were what is considered in dog terminology "long and low" (i.e., short on leg and long in body). Those who were recipients of these imports were convinced they represented the best of what Europe had to offer at the time. There were others of us who wondered, if in fact, the early imports were the best of what was available or if they simply represented what European fanciers were inclined to part with at that time.

Those of us who had had experience with importing dogs, sight unseen, from foreign countries were aware the best of what a country has to offer is not always what is exported. Even if "the best available" at a given time is sent, it does not necessarily follow that this represents the breed ideal. There was no way to know if this was so in the case of the early Bichon imports.

Regardless, it was apparent standardization was critical in determining what was meant by "body." Most canine anatomy experts agree that in dog terminology body refers to the entire body—from forward most to rear most—in other words, sternum to buttocks.

Even agreement in this area could not fully resolve the problem of proportions. We were still saddled with the words "slightly longer" and the varied interpretation of just what that meant. Just how much was "slightly?"

Finding the Key

Surprisingly we were to find all the answers to the problem in the original French standard of the breed. The reason the answer had eluded discovery

Photo by Ashbey

was that it was tucked away in the standard's description of "crest," or neck. That portion of the standard read as follows: *"Its (the neck's) length is approximately one-third the length of the body, the proportion being about four-and-one-half inches to thirteen and-one-half inches for a subject eleven inches high."*

In other words, the original standard called for a body length of 13.5 inches for a subject that measured 11 inches tall. This gave us a ratio of 22.5% additional body length when compared to height at shoulder. Therefore, there was no way possible to achieve this body ratio if one used the measuring point of highest point of shoulder to set on of tail as body length.

Unfortunately, these important findings were not met with the unanimous approval we had anticipated. There was marked resistance from the advocates of the longer cast dog. Their eye had become accustomed to this style and the new discovery appeared more as a threat to what they believed to be correct that any significant step forward.

In all fairness, it should be understood their resistance arose from a fear that these proportions put the Bichon Frise at risk of assuming the Poodle's proportions. What they were not taking into consideration was the fact that these these calculations still gave the Bichon over 20% more body length than the Poodle— easily considered a serious departure from correct Poodle construction.

It was important to the breed that this area be correctly defined, but there was more at stake. The BFCA was in the midst of working on a revision directed toward clarifying the standard's ambiguities. It was not the time to destroy the spirit of cooperation that had existed within the BFCA since its inception. A way had to be found to bring the proportions around to approximate what they should be without alienating important members. There were a good number of other items in the standard that would take compromise, it did not seem worth while to come to a stalemate over just one of them.

The surest way to incur opposition to this new-found proportion information was to suggest the

Photo by Lucas Studio, Virginia Beach, Virginia.

Bichon had a "short back" (withers to tail set). Yet, at the same time, the body length of an additional 22.5% seemed fully acceptable. Though it was anatomically impossible to have the correct body length and a well laid back shoulder without a back that was shorter than the dog was tall, it was obvious that if any movement was to be made in this area it had to be made gradually.

First things first. Setting what actually constituted the breed's body and giving it a maximum length were the important first steps. The most that could be done at that point in regard to back length was to bring it around to some modicum of what it should actually be without specifically *stating* what it actually should be.

There was only one way around the problem. Create a silhouette that resulted in a body length that was correct but have it illustrate a back that squared with the dog's height. Anatomically impossible of course but it would provide the first step toward the breed attaining its true proportions.

This sham silhouette first appeared in the *Bichon Frise Workbook* which was written in 1975. I knew this impossible-to-achieve outline would one day come back to haunt us. At the time though, I could not help but reflect upon the truth in the old adage, "a camel is indeed a horse designed by a committee." It did, however, accomplish what we set out to do—maintain the spirit of cooperation that prevailed in the breed and take us at least one step closer toward uniformity.

A far more definitive breed standard was drafted and approved by the AKC in December of 1979 but body proportions outside of the old "slightly longer than tall" were still not addressed. However, everything else within the correct silhouette was attended to and that standard helped pave the way for the time when those within the breed were ready to give a more definitive interpretation to the all-important height-length proportions.

Typical of the Bichon's indomitable history, the breed survived our inability to come to terms with definitions. The breed not only survived but flourished - here in America and around the world. It had become a breed to be reckoned with.

Much of the breed's progress was recorded in the 1982 work, *The Bichon Frise Today*. Throughout Canada, Great Britain, Scandinavia, Australia and New Zealand the Bichon Frise was demanding attention. America had taken the little "street dog," given it a bath, a haircut and a sparkling new image that appealed to breeders and exhibitors throughout the world. It became the dog of the 80s!

While full credit must be given to the pioneers of the breed throughout the world, it is the Bichon itself that ultimately has earned the wonderful place of distinction it has. Were it not for Michael Coad's Ch. Tiopeppi Mad Louie at Pamplona in England, Azara Kennel's Ch. Jazz de la Buthiere of Leijazulip in Australia and Phyllis Tabler's Ch. Chaminade Syncopation in the U.S., the dog world might never have known what a great show dog the happy little Bichon could be.

The World Congresses

While judging at the Scottish Kennel Club in May of 1986 I met Pauline Block, Secretary of the Bichon Frise Club of Great Britain, Pauline Block and breeder-exhibitors Den Thomas and Stephen Thompson. We all became fast friends and shared our hopes and concerns for the breed.

Mrs. Block proved to be a fascinating individual whose success in many breeds had given her almost legendary status in the United Kingdom. Thomas and Thompson well represented the opposite end of the spectrum—the young, extremely enthusiastic and highly successful new fancier. Our widely diversified backgrounds helped to contribute to what would eventually prove to be historic moment in the breed as it led to the idea for a International Bichon Frise Congress. A quick call to Barbara Stubbs in the U.S. before I left Great Britain convinced us the idea was a sound one and the groundwork for the first Congress had been laid.

In the interim the BFCA was notified by the AKC that all breed parent clubs were being called upon to standardize the formats of their official breed standards. It was the AKC's intent that there would be some consistency in where information would appear within all the standards and in the terminology used.

The BFCA immediately set to work and in the end produced one of the best written and most accurately descritive of the AKC breed standards. The new standard addressed proportions definitively and accurately. The single omission, however, was that which addressed length of back.

The first Congress was held in London in February of 1988 in conjunction with the famed Crufts Dog Show with the Bichon Frise Club of Great Britain acting as host. In attendance were diehard fanciers from around the world. Their dedication and enthusiasm brought them together to learn what their fellow fanciers were accomplishing and to offer assistance in providing for the welfare of the breed.

Among the many significant topics discussed over the days of the Congress was the desire on all our parts to develop as much uniformity in the breed as possible while still allowing for the minor differences each country felt appropriate.

A major point of discussion at most canine World Congresses, that of developing international breed standards, was also briefly discussed. We agreed that although the topic occupied many, many hours on the agendas of these other congresses, time had proven International Standards were not only an exercise in futility they were unnecessary. If major fanciers could come to common agreement on what constituted the "essence" of a breed, years of argument on whose standard said it best would be eliminated.

Although some question had existed regarding the attitude of the Bichon fanciers world-wide toward showing the Bichon brushed and trimmed, it was forever resolved at the First World Congress. The entire Congress body of 160 members representing 15 countries in which the Bichon Frise was being shown voted unanimously to adopt the style of presentation being used in the United States.

The Congress fully credited France and Belgium as the Bichon Frise's countries of origin and desig-

nated America as the country of development. The latter based upon the resurrection of the breed from obscurity by American fanciers and the subsequent rebirth of interest in the breed around the world.

Closing in accord as to the success and benefits of the Congress, the Bichon Frise Club of New South Wales, representing Australia, put forward an offer to host the next congress in 1993. Their offer was unanimously accepted.

The 1993 Congress was held in Sydney, Australia, again attracting dedicated fanciers from around the world. The well organized Congress helped to renew old friendships and establish new ones. As it had in London, the gathering also gave international visitors the opportunity of seeing what progress had been made in the breed in a country most had only hitherto read about. The Australians proved themselves both knowledgeable and capable of producing a Bichon that could make contributions to breeding programs the world over.

Undoubtedly one of the more significant accomplishments of the second congress was the ratification of a statement defining the international "essence of the breed." It appears here as originally read and agreed upon in 1993.

The Essence of the Breed

The Bichon Frise is a substantial dog typified by its exquisite balance and proportion. Its white, powder-puff of a coat is rounded off from any direction. Internationally, ideal size falls between ten and eleven-and-one-half inches. The Bichon is slightly shorter in back than it is high at the withers while the body (pronounced forechest to buttocks) is slightly longer than height at the withers. The elegantly long neck is arched into well laid-back shoulders which are complimented by well-angulated rear quarters permitting movement with easy reach and drive. Its mischievous dark-eyed expression is accentuated by jet black pigmentation.

Temperament is always merry and bright, evidenced by the jaunty over-the-back carriage of its tail and happy-go-lucky attitude.

The BFCA sent copies of its newly published *Illustrated Discussion of the Bichon Frise Standard* to the Australian congress. it was particularly significant in that it analyzed the standard in complete detail and was the first time the historic evasion of length of back was dealt with. The *Illustrated Discussion* stated clearly, "Given these correct proportions as stated in the standard, it would then follow that the measurement from withers to tail, generally referred to an length of back, would be shorter than the dog's height - approximately 1/4 less than height at withers."

The camaraderie and knowledge gained brought the successful congress to a close with the offer from the United States to hold the Third International Congress in Los Angeles, California in 1998.

As those attending the Australian Congress reflected on the many benefits on their return journeys home, there was no doubt in anyone's mind that the breed had certainly met the expectations of those original 28 members of the BFCA - perhaps even exceeded them. Their faith in the little white dogs from the Continent had been realized.

THE FOUR BICHON VARIETIES

Bichon Bolognaise

Bichon Havanese

Bichon Teneriffe (nee Frise)

Bichon Maltaise

Today's Maltese. The outstanding winner, Ch. Sand Island Small Kraft Lite. Controversy exists as to whether or not the modern Maltese descends from the old Bichon Maltaise. The Bolognaise bitch pictured above is UKC and ARBA Ch. Berdot's Sophia of Assisi owned by Kristine Steffeck.

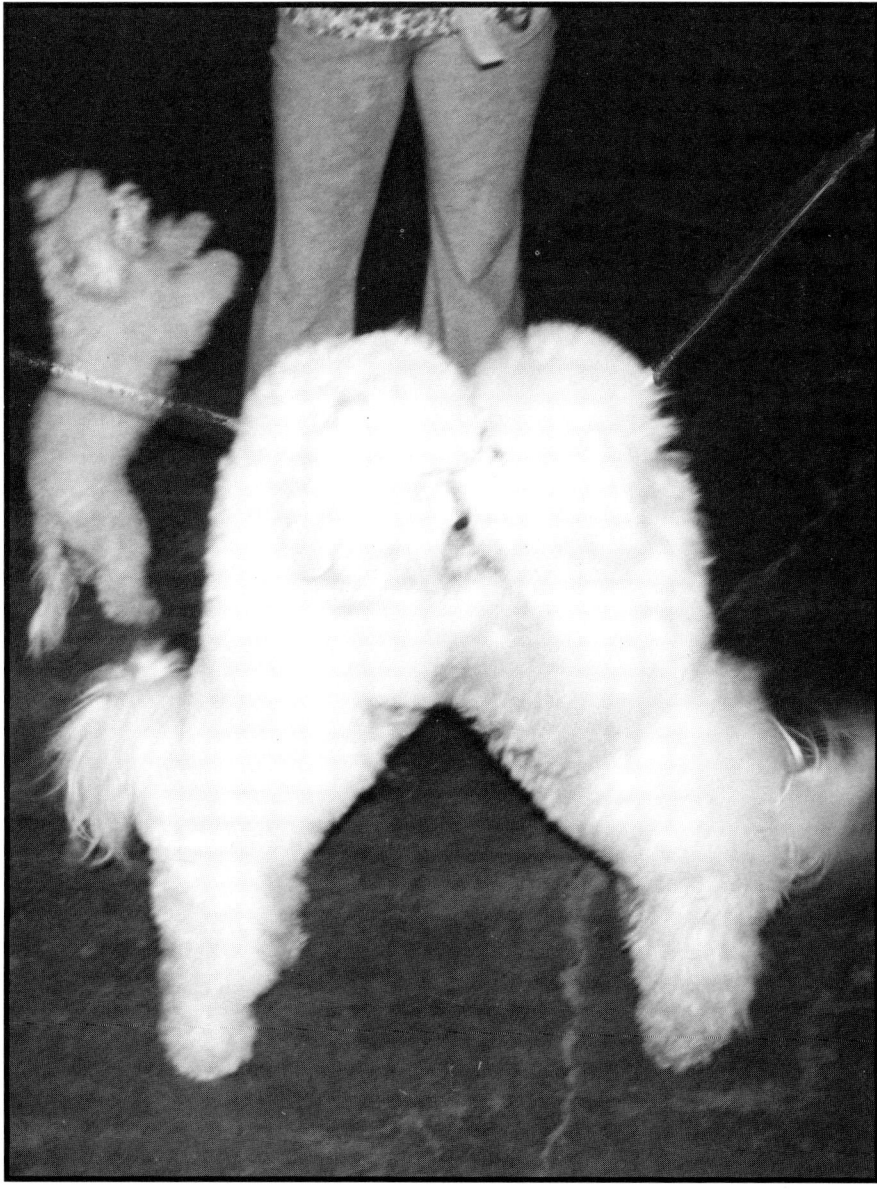

The Bichon's inate ability to walk and dance on its hind legs still exists in the breed today as is demonstrated by the trio above photographed in 1972.

BFCA'S PIONEER MEMBERS

Azalea Gascoigne

Gertrude Fournier

Mayree Butler

Early imports: Lassy of Milton and Etoile King of Rayita (right). Dapper Dan de Gascoigne (lower right) pictured completing his Mexican championship under judge, Derek Rayne. Handled by Jack Dougherty for owner, Mayree Butler. Barbara Stubbs (the famous "Lady in Black") and her son, Bruce Stubbs (below). The two did much to bring the Bichon to the attention of America's exhibiting fancy. (Missy photo)

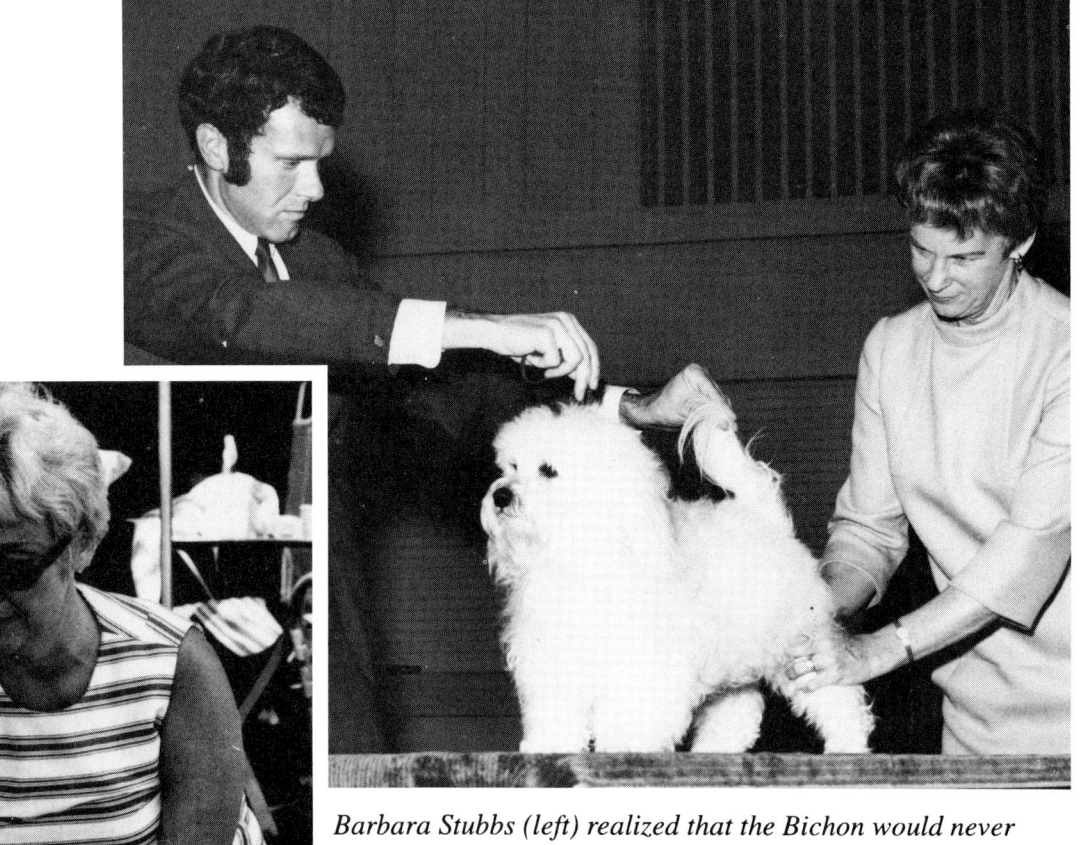
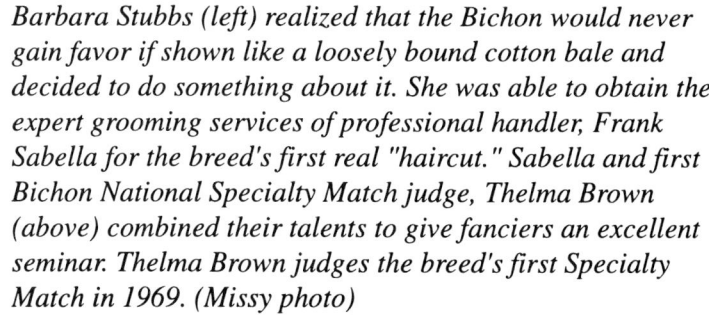

Barbara Stubbs (left) realized that the Bichon would never gain favor if shown like a loosely bound cotton bale and decided to do something about it. She was able to obtain the expert grooming services of professional handler, Frank Sabella for the breed's first real "haircut." Sabella and first Bichon National Specialty Match judge, Thelma Brown (above) combined their talents to give fanciers an excellent seminar. Thelma Brown judges the breed's first Specialty Match in 1969. (Missy photo)

Rick Beauchamp sees his first Bichons and takes the very young champion-to-be Chaminade Sonata into the ring. Sonata was litter sister to Ch. Chaminade Mr. Beau Monde and she was to become the dam of Ch. Chaminade Syncopation, the breed's first all breed Best in Show winner. Bruce Stubbs (right) and one of the breed's most influential producers. Ch. Reenroy's Ami du Kilkanny. Her head and expression as well as overall type was to set the style for the entire breed. (Missy photo) Ch. Chaminade Sonata, Ch. Chaminade Mr. Beau Monde (then known as Chaminade Capriccio) and their brother, Chaminade Fortissimo pictured at 8 weeks. (Missy photo)

Betty White gave the breed its first national exposure on her syndicated TV show "Pet Set" (above). As the 70's got under way those seriously involved with the breed felt it was time to begin to create some explanatory literature for Bichons. Thus, the first known work on the breed, "The Bichon Frise Handbook" by Richard Beauchamp (left). Proportions and presentation varied wildly in the breed and general consensus was that both had to be standardized. In 1972 champion-to-be Stardom's Odin Rex, Jr. won the Virginia Rare Breeds show in the "natural" style of the day. He was owned and handled by Stella Raabe.

AKC RECOGNIZES THE BICHON

The BFCA held its annual Specialty Match the day before the Bichon's first day as a recognized breed which was April 8, 1973. There were probably as many famous professional handlers showing the breed as one would see at the specialties of the most established breeds. Jane Forsyth (top left) who was to become one of the breed's most successful handlers. Ted Young, Jr. (above) with Chaminade Syncopation. Mike Dougherty (left) with Cali-Col's Scalawag, the Best of Breed winner at both the Specialty Match and at Silver State KC the following day. (Ludwig photo)

Ch. Chaminade Syncopation ("Snidely Whiplash") wins the historic first all breed Best In Show for Bichons on May 7, 1973 at Framington Valley KC under judge, Mr. Louis Murr. Snidely was handled by Ted Young, Jr. for owners Mr. & Mrs. William Tabler.

BICHON FRISE TOPS FARMINGTON SHOW

First Recognition for New Breed From France

Special to The New York Times

FARMINGTON, Conn., July 7, - Louis J. Murr, who has judged dogs for 51 years and is one of the few licensed American Kennel Club judges eligible to judge any of the 116 recognized breeds, chose a Bichon Frise yesterday as best in show.

The newly recognized dog was selected at the 25th anniversary of the Farmington Valley Kennel Club, where 1,500 dogs were exhibited on the grounds of the Farmington Valley Polo Club.

The Bichon, Ch. Chaminade's Syncopation, a white, medium-size animal weighing about 15 pounds, was shown by Ted Young. The dog was bred by Dick Beauchamp and Barbara B. Stubbs and is owned by Mrs. William Tabler of Glen Head, Long Island.

Chaminade is 18 months old and has never been beaten - before the breed was recognized in April - and has won sever nonsporting groups.

Murr commented: "This is the finest Bichon I have ever seen in this or any other country." The breed is of French ancestry. Murr added, "It is put down in perfect coat and asked for it by knowing exactly what was expected of him."

The Empire Saluki Club specialty winner was a class dog called Misruie's Nicholas owned by Charles R. Dear.

Ch. C & D Beau Monde Sunbeam becomes the first Bichon Frise bitch to win an all breed Best In Show. The event took place on March 20, 1974 at the Longview KC (Texas) under judge, Winifred Heckman. She was shown by Joe Waterman for her owner, George Ann Slocum. (Toomey photo)

The first Best of Breed winner at Westminster KC (February 1974) was Robert Koeppel's Ch. Rank's Eddie. The judge was Melbourne T.L. Downing and the handler was Richard Bauer. (Kennel Review photo) Getting ready (lower photo) for the first National Specialty show for the breed (from far left): Marvel Brown, Mary Vogel, Waterman assistant and Joe & Pauline Waterman. (MikRon photo)

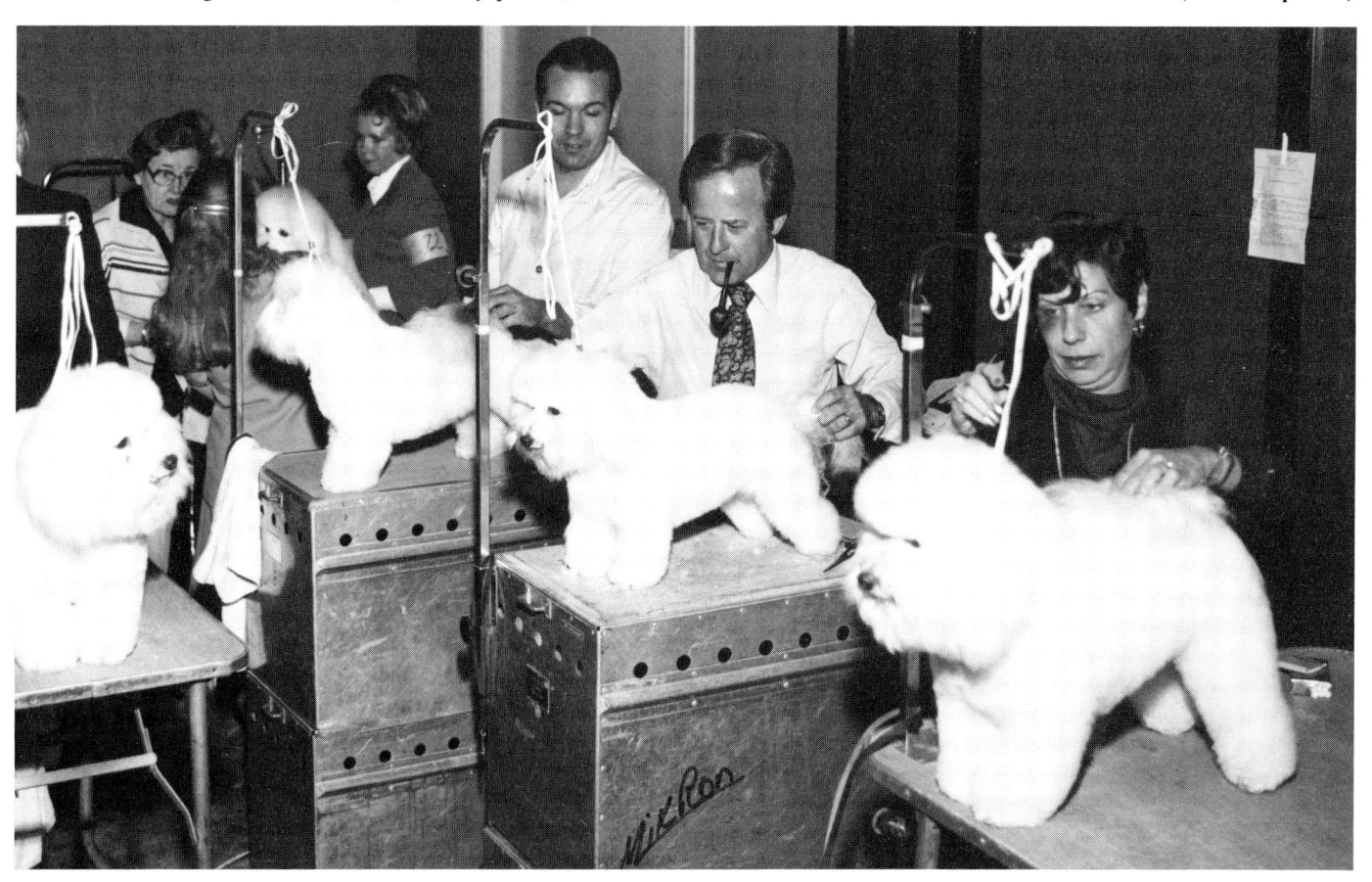

Ch. Vogelflight's Music Man wins the first National Specialty under judge Langdon Skarda. Handled by Joe Waterman for owners Nan and Burt Busk.

Ch. Cali-Col's Villanelle (Best Opposite Sex to Best of Breed) owned by Gene & Mary Ellen Mills was the only major winner at the first National Specialty who was not either sired by or grandsired by Ch. Chaminade Mr. Beau Monde. Handled here by Jeannine Walker. (Villanelle was bred to Mr. Beau Monde immediately adfter the judging of that show.) (Missy photo)

All in the family at the first National: Best Veteran, Ch. Cali-Col's Robspierre; Best Stud Dog, Robspierre's son, Ch. Chaminade Mr. Beau Monde; Best of Breed, Mr. Beau Monde's son, Ch. Vogelflight's Music Man; Winners Bitch, Best Winners, Mr. Beau Monde's daughter, Ch. C & D Beau Monde Moonshine. (Missy photo)

The Chaminade Trio: Ch. Cali-Col's Robspierre, Ch. Reenroy's Ami du Kilkanny and Ch. Petit Galant de St. George. Their influence upon the breed may never be duplicated. (Missy photo)

DETERMINING PROPORTIONS

Ch. Beau Monde the Brat pictured completing her championship. Were her proportions what the standard really asked for?   (Petrulis photo)

Ch. Jalwin Pattern of Paw Mark, a contemporary of The Brat. How could both be correct?   (Ludwig photo)

Ch. Devon's Puff and Stuff becomes the top winning Bichon Frise of all time with 60 all breed Bests In Show, Best of Breed at two consecutive Nationals and twice winner of the Non Sporting Group at the Westmindter KC. Handled by Michael Kemp for breeder, owner, Nancy Shapland. *(Petrulis photo)*

THE BICHON RECROSSES THE ATLANTIC

Am.Ch. Vogelflights Choir Boy of Leander (litter brother to Ch. Vogelflight's Music Man) startles England by taking Reserve Best in Show at the famed Bath all breed championship show in 1977. This win from a class that would be considered similiar to the AKC's Miscellaneous Class, an almost unheard of accomplishment. (Lionel Young photo)

Ch. Tiopepi Mad Louie at Pamplona pictured at Crufts. Louie's outstanding proportions and type, combined with the grooming expertise of the Corish-Coad team convinced England that "the American way" was certainly the way to proceed. The late Catherine Sutton, one of England's most famed all breed judges, and Richard Beauchamp did everything in their power to create a breeding between America's Puff and Stuff and Mad Louie but England's quarantine laws made it impossible.
Mad Louie shown on the left with handler Geoff Corish and judge Richard Beauchamp at Scottish Kennel Club. Louie's winning ways and marvelous temperament earned the breed a permanent position of respect among English fanciers of all breeds. He was owned by Michael Coad.
(D.J.Lindsay photo)

Author, Richard Beauchamp in England pictured with Steven Thompson handling Ch. Roushkas Song and Dance and Den Thomas handling Ch. Roushka's Dance Master. (D. Freeman)

Again proving how similar Bichon type is from country to country is Mrs. B. Dickinson's English bred Ch. Hylacer Northern Topic (left), a Mad Louie son.

Right, a Swedish bred charmer showing what lovely heads are being bred there.

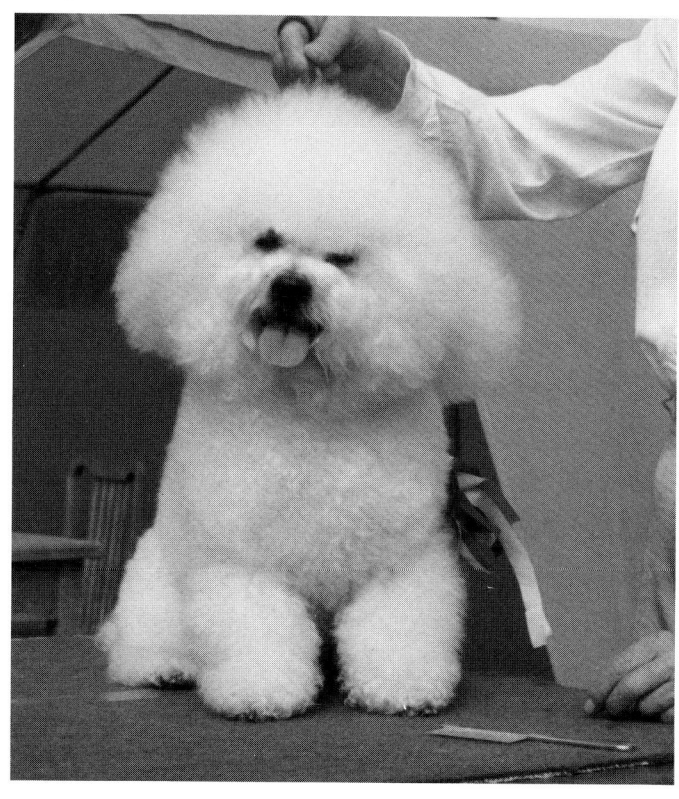

Above, another Swedish bred youngster with the proportions and elegance that would make breeders anywhere green with envy. There is little doubt that Finland is producing Bichons capable of competing anywhere in the world. This pair (right) were the author's winning dog, Fin.Den.Ch. Jitterbop Cradle of Love (Best of Breed) and bitch, Ch. Jitterbop Joy & Pride (Best Opposite Sex) at the Helsinki show in Finland.

Ch. Beau Monde Cameo Call Boy (below), bred by Ginger Le Cave, completed his American, Danish and European International Championships before returning and retiring in America. A seriously overlooked dog who undoubtedly had one of the best constructed fronts and rears of any other American bred dog. He was a strong influence throughout several European and Scandinavian countries and produced champions here in America as well.   (Wesseltoft photo)

MORE BICHONS FROM ACROSS THE SEAS

Australian Ch. Jazz de la Buthiere of Leijazulip's beautiful head and excellent pigment were only part of the reason this top winning dog had such a great influence in Australia. His winning ways and quality offspring helped pave the way for the breed in his home country. Jazz was owned by Azara Kennels.

Bred and campaigned in Japan, this extremely typey young bitch is an excellent representative for the breed in the Orient.

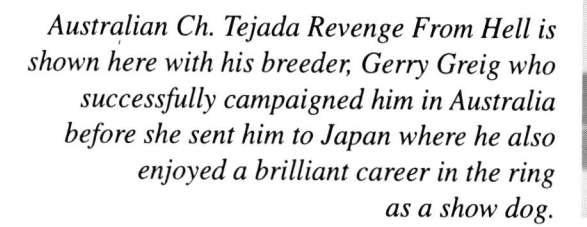

Australian Ch. Tejada Revenge From Hell is shown here with his breeder, Gerry Greig who successfully campaigned him in Australia before she sent him to Japan where he also enjoyed a brilliant career in the ring as a show dog.

BFCA NATIONAL SPECIALTY BEST OF BREED WINNERS
1976 - 1997

1976	**CH. VOGELFLIGHT'S MUSIC MAN**	Breeder: M. Vogel. Owner: V. Busk
1977	**CH. VOGELFLIGHT'S MUSIC MAN**	Breeder: M. Vogel. Owner: V. Busk
1978	**CH. VOGELFLIGHT'S MUSIC MAN**	Breeder: M. Vogel. Owner: V. Busk
1979	**CH. BEAU MONDE THE ICE MAN**	Breeder: R. Beauchamp & P. Craig. Owner: Mrs. C. Porter
1980	**CH. CROCKERLY BEAU MONDE ECLIPSE**	Breeders: R. & J. Blood. Owner: N. Shapland
1981	**CH. RANK'S RAGGEDY ANDY**	Breeders: J. Rank & J. Thayer. Owner: N. Makowiec
1982	**CH. JALWIN JUST A JIFFY**	Breeder: A. Hearn. Owners: M. & P. Schultz
1983	**CH. HILLWOOD BRASS BAND**	Breeder: E. Iverson. Owner: E. MacNeill
1984	**CH. CAMELOT'S BRASSY NICKEL**	Breeder-owner: P. Goldman
1985	**CH. DEVON PUFF AND STUFF**	Breeder-owner: N. Shapland
1986	**CH. DEVON PUFF AND STUFF**	Breeder-owner: N. Shapland
1987	**CH. ALPENGLOW ASHLEY DU CHAMOUR**	Breeder: B. Stubbs & L. Day. Owner: J. McClaran
1988	**CH. PARFAIT HELLSAPOPPIN OF DRUID**	Breeder: J. Spilman. Owners: J. Spilman L. Kilduff, T. Lao, B. Beatley
1989	**CH. CHAMINADE LE BLANC CHAMOUR**	Breeders: L. Morrow, B. Stubbs, G. & H. Harrell Owners: L. Morrow, C. & R. Vida
1990	**CH. CHAMINADE LE BLANC CHAMOUR**	Breeders: L. Morrow, B. Stubbs, G. & H. Harrell Owners: L. Morrow & C. & R. Vida
1991	**CH. SEA STAR'S BEAU BRUMMEL**	Breeder: J. Cohen. Owners: J. Cohen & B. Thomas
1992	**CH. CHAMINADE LARKSHIRE LAFITTE**	Breeders-owners: J. O'Day, B. Stubbs & L. Morrow
1993	**CH. CHAMINADE LARKSHIRE LAFITTE**	Breeders-owners: J. O'Day, B. Stubbs & L. Morrow
1994	**CH. SPELLBOUND'S PANACHE**	Breeder: B.B. Barton. Owners: B.B. Barton & J. & P. Kee
1995	**CH. GOLD COAST SAKS JACKPOT**	Breeders: J. Pearce, L. Dickens & S. Chantelois. Owners: S. & K. Hanson
1996	**CH. CRAIGDALE YOANNEWYN EL TORO**	Breeder: D. Hunter. Owner: L. Morrow
1997	**CH. STERLING RUMOR HAS IT**	Breeders: P. Flores, S. Swartz & N. Mitchell Owners: M. Tamaki & P. Flores

Ch. Chaminade Syncopation (the great "Snidely Whiplash.")

Chapter II
TRANSITION OF THE STANDARDS

THE FRENCH STANDARD OF THE BREED
Adapted by the Societe Centrale Canune of France
March 5, 1933

GENERAL APPEARANCE: A little dog, gay and joyful, with a medium size muzzle and long hair curling loosely. Dark eyes are bright and expressive. Viewed from the side giving a slightly roached appearance.

HEAD: The cranium is larger than the nose and will measure approximately from two inches to three and one-half inches, the circumference of the cranium corresponding to the height of the withers, about ten and one-half inches.

LIPS: Fine, somewhat dry but less than the Schipperke, never drooping and heavy, they are normally pigmented black, the lower lip should not be heavy or noticeable but should not be soft and not let the mucous membrane show when the mouth is closed.

DENTURE: Normal, the fore teeth of the lower jaw should be against and behind the points of the upper teeth. (scissors).

MUZZLE: Should not be thick and heavy but not pinched. The cheeks are flat and not muscular, the stop accentuated slightly.

EYES: Dark, as much as possible surrounded by black, are rather round and not almond shaped. They should not be placed at an oblique angle, are lively, not too large, not showing any white when looking forward. They should not sag and the eye globe should not bulge in an exaggerated manner.

CRANIUM: Rather flat to the touch although the fur gives a round appearance.

EARS: Drooping, well covered with long wavy hair. Carried rather forward when at attention, the length of the cartilage can not reach the truffle as the French Poodle but only half way the length of the muzzle. In fact, they are not large and are finer than those of the Poodle.

CREST (or neck): Rather long. Carried highly and proudly, it is round and fine, close to the cranium, widening gradually to meet the withers. Its length is appoximately one-third the length of the body (proportion being about four and one half inches to thirteen and one-half inches for a subject eleven inches high).

WITHERS: Are rather oblique, not prominent, giving the appearance of being as long as the forearm, approximately four inches. Forearm should not be spread out from the body and the elbow, in particular, should not point outward.

LEGS: Are straight when looking from the front, of good standing, of fine bones; the pastern short and straight when viewed trom the front, very slightly oblique from the profile view, the toe nails should be black by preference, but it is difficult to obtain.

CHEST: Well developed, the sternum is pronounced, the lower ribs rather round and not ending abruptly, the chest being horizontally rather deep. The flanks are close to the belly, the skin is fine and not floating.

LOIN: Large and muscular. The hock is more elbowed than the Poodle

TAIL: Is normally carried upwards and graciously curved over the dorsal spine. The hair of thc tail is long and will lay on the back.

PIGMENTATION: Under the white hair is preferably dark. The sexual organs are also pigmented black, bluish or beige, as are the spots often found on the body.

COLOR: Preferably all white, sometimes white with tan or gray on the ears and body. HAIR: Should be fine, silky and loosely curled, its length being approximately two and one-half inches to four inches long. Unlike the Maltese the Bichon Frise also has an under coat.

SIZE: The height of the withers can not be over twelve inches the smaller the dog being the element of success.

REASON FOR DISQUALIFICATION: **Inferior prognathism, pink nose, flesh colored lips, pale eyes, tail curled in a cork-screw manner, black spots in the fur. ** Weight should not exceed eleven (11) pounds.

(From the pamphlet, "LETS EXAMINE OUR BREED STANDARD!", published by the Bichon Frise Club of America in 1967).

F.C.I. STANDARD OF THE CURLYHAIRED BICHON
(Bichon A 'Poil Frise')

GENERAL CHARACTERISTICS A small, gay, playful dog, with a lively galt, a muzzle of moderate length, long hair in a corkscrew curl. The hair is very slack and is something like that of the Mongolian goat. The head is carried proudly and high, the dark eyes are vivacious and expressive.

SIZE Height at withers: must not go beyond 12 inches, the small size being an element of success in show.

HEAD The skull is longer than the muzzle in the ratio of 8 to 5; the circumference of the skull is approximately equal to the height at the withers. The nose is rounded, definitely black, smooth and glossy. The lips are thin, fairly lean, although not quite like the Schipperke (q.v.), falling just far enough to cover the lower lips but never heavy or pendulous. The lips are normally black; the lower lip must not be heavy or obvious, nor can it be slack. The inner area must not be visible when thc mouth is closed. The mouth is neither undershot nor overshot, the jaws meeting in a scissors bite. The muzzle should be neither thick nor heavy, but it must not be pinched. The cheeks are flat, not very muscular. The skull is rather flat to the touch, although the coat gives it a rounded appearance.

EYES Dark as possible, with dark eye rims. They are rather rounded, not almond-shaped. They are lively and set straight, i.e., not obliquely. The whites do not show. The eyes are lively but are neither large nor prominent as in the Brussels Griffon or the Pekingese. The socket does not bulge, nor do the eyes.

EARS Drooping, well furnished with crisp, long hair carried rather forward on alert, but in such a way that the fore edge touches the skull. They should not reach the tip of the nose when exterlded, as in the Poodle, but should go just about halfway. Besides, they are not as wide and fine as a Poodle's.

NECK Fairly long and carried high and proudly. Round and slender near the skull, it broadens gradually and fits smoothly into the shoulders. Lengthwise, it measures about a third of the body.

BODY The chest is well develped, the sternum is pronounced. The back ribs are rounded and do not terminate abruptly, thus giving a substantial horizontal depth to the chest. The flanks are well tucked up at the belly; the skin at that point is thin. The loin is wide and well muscled, slightly arched. The pelvis is wide, the rump slightly rounded.

TAIL Normally the tail is carried high and gracerully curved in line with the spine without actually being rolled up. It is not docked and must not be close to the back, although the hair may fall against the backline. It is set on slightly lower than in the Poodle,

FOREQUARTERS The shoulder is fairly slanting, not prom inent, and gives the appearance of being about the same length as the forearm (about 4 inches). The foreleg is not turned ol-tward from the IJody, especially at the elbow. The legs, viewed from the front, must be straight and finely boned; in profile they are very slightly slanting.

HINDQUARTERS The thighs are wide, well muscled anrl with thc legs well slarlTed. The hock is also more angulated than is the case with the Poodle.

FEET Black nails are preferred, although this ideal is hard to attain.

COAT The hair is fine, silky and crisply curled, 3-4 inches long, and neither flat nor ropy.

COLOR The ideal is pure white, although tan or dark gray markings are permissible on the ears and body. The dog may be shown with only the feet and muzzle clipped.

SKIN The pigmentation beneath the coat is preferably dark, and if so the genitals are either black, bluish, or beige, depending on the body markings.

FAULTS Pigmentation extending into the hair and forming spots; flat, wavy, roped or too short hair; monorchidism; overshot or undershot jaw; failure to meet standards for height and length.

DISQUALIFICATIONS Undershot or overshot jaw to the extent that incisors do not touch; pink nose; flesh-colored lips; pale eyes; cryptorchidism; tail rolled up or spiraled; black spots on coat.

OFFICIAL BICHON FRISE STANDARD
Accepted by vote of the Bichon Frise Club of America membership
September, 1968

1 - GENERAL APPEARANCE—A sturdy, lively dog of stable temperament, with a stylish gait and an air of dignity and intelligence.

2 - COLOR—Solid white, or white with cream, apricot, or grey on the ears and/or body.

3 - HEAD—Proportionate to the size of the dog. Skull broad and somewhat round, but not coarse, covered with a topknot of hair.

4 - MUZZLE—Of medium length, not heavy or snipey. Slightly accentuated stop.

5 - EARS—Dropped, covered with long flowing hair. The leather should reach approximately halfway the length of the muzzle.

6 - EYES—Black or dark brown, with black rims. Large, round, expressive, and alert.

7 - LIPS—Black, fine, never drooping.

8 - NOSE—Black round, pronounced.

9 - BITE—Scissors.

10 - NECK—Rather long, and gracefully and proudly carried behind an erect head.

11 - SHOULDERS—Well laid back. Elbows held close to the body .

12 - BODY—Slightly longer than tall. Well developed with good spring of ribs. The back inclines gradually from the withers to a slight rise over the loin. The loin is large and muscular. The brisket, well let down.

13 - TAIL—Covered with long flowing hair, carried gaily and curved to lie on the back.

14 - SIZE—The height at the withers should not exceed 12 inches nor be under 8 inches.

15 - LEGS & FEET—Strong boned, appearing straight, with well knit pasterns. Hindquarters well angulated. Feet, resembling cat's paws are tight and round.

16 - COAT—Profuse, silky and loosely curled. There is an undercoat.

17 - GROOMING—Scissored to show the eyes and to give a full, rounded appearance to the head and body. Feet should have hair trimmed to give a rounded appearance. When properly brushed, there is an overall "powder puff" appearance. Puppies may be shown in short coat, but the minimum show coat for an adult is two inches.

18 - FAULTS—Cowhocks, snipey muzzle, poor pigmentation, protruding eyes, yellow eyes, undershot or overshot bite, corkscrew tail, black hair in the coat.

REVISED STANDARD FOR THE BICHON FRISE
Approved December 11, 1979

GENERAL APPEARANCE - The Bichon Frise is a small, sturdy, white powder puff of a dog whose merry temperament is evidenced by his plumed tail carried jauntily over the back and his dark eyed inquisitive expression. Coming and going, his movement is precise and true. In profile he measures the same from withers to ground as from withers to set of tail. The body from the forward most point of the sternum to the buttocks is slightly longer than height at the withers. He moves with steady topline and easy reach and drive.

HEAD - The head is covered with a topknot of hair that creates an overall rounded impression. The skull is slightly rounded allowing for a round and foward looking eye. A properly balanced head is three parts muzzle to five parts skull, measured from the nose to the slightly accentuated stop and from stop to occiput; a line drawn between the outside corners of the eyes and to the nose will create a near equilateral triangle. There is a slight degree of chiseling under the eyes, but not so much as to result in a weak or snipey foreface. The lower jaw is strong.

Nose - is prominent and always black.

Teeth - meet in a scissors bite. An undershot or overshot jaw should be severely penalized. A crooked or out of line tooth is permissable, however, missing teeth are to be severely faulted.

Eyes - are round, black or dark brown and are set in the skull to look directly forward. An overly large or bulging eye is a fault as is an almond shaped, obliquely set eye. Halos, the black or very dark brown skin surrounding the eyes, are necessary as they accentuate the eye and enhance expression. The eye rims themselves must be black. Broken pigment or total absence of pigment on the eye rims produce a blank and staring expression which is a definite fault. Yellow, blue or grey eyes are a serious fault and should be severely penalized.

Ears - are dropped and are covered with long flowing hair. When extended toward the nose, the leathers should reach ap proximately halfway the length of the muzzle. They are set on slightly higher than eye level and rather foward on the skull, so that when the dog is alerted they serve to frame the face.

Lips - are black, fine, never drooping.

NECK AND BODY

Neck - The arched neck is long and carried proudly and gracefully behind an erect head. It blends smoothly into the shoulders. The length of neck from occiput to withers is approximately one third the distance from sternum to buttocks.

Body - The topline is level except for a slight arch over the loin.

Sternum - is well pronounced and protrudes slightly forward of the point of shoulder.

Chest - is well developed and wide enough to allow free and unrestricted forward movement of the front legs.

Ribcage - is moderately sprung and extends back to a short and muscular loin.

Tail - is well plumed, set on level with the topline and is curved gracefully over the back so that the hair of the tail rests on the back. A low tail set, a tail carried perpendicularly to the back, or a tail which droops behind should be severely penalized. When the tail is extended toward the head it should reach at least half way to the withers. A corkscrew tail is a very serious tault.

FOREQUARTERS

Shoulders - The shoulder blade, upper arm and forearm should be approximately equal in length. The shoulders are laid back to somewhat near a forty-five degree angle. The upper arm extends well back so the elbow is placed directly below the withers when viewed from the side.

Legs - should be of medium bone, not too fine or too coarse, straight with no bow or curve in the forearm or wrist. The elbows are held close to the body.

Pasterns - slope slightly from the vertical.

Feet - are tight and round resembling those of a cat and point directly forward, turning neither in nor out.

Pads - are black.

Nails - are kept short, the dew claws may be removed.

Hindquarters - are of medium bone, well angulated with muscular thighs and spaced moderately wide. The upper and lower thigh are nearly equal in length meeting at a well bent stifle joint. The leg from hock joint to foot pad is perpendicular to the ground. Paws are tight and round with black pads. Dewclaws may be removed. Cowhocks are a very serious fault.

COAT

Texture - of the coat is of utmost importance. The undercoat is soft and dense, the outercoat of a coarser and curlier texture. The combination of the two gives a soft but substantial feel to the touch which is similar to plush or velvet and when patted springs back. When bathed and brushed it stands off the body, creating an overall powder puff appearance. A wirey coat is not desirable. A silky coat is a fault. A coat that lies down and lack of undercoat are very serious faults.

Trimming - The coat is trimmed to reveal the natural outline of the body. It is rounded off from any direction and never cut so short as to create an overly trimmed or squared off appearance. The furnishings of the head, beard, moustache, ears and tail are left longer. The topline should be trimmed to appear level. The coat should be long enough to maintain the powder puff look which is characteristic of the breed.

Color - is white, may have shadings of buff, cream, or apricot around the ears or on the body. Any color in excess of 10% of the entire coat of a mature specimen is a fault and should be penalized, but color of the accepted shadings should not be faulted in puppies.

Gait - Movement at a trot is free, precise and effortless. In profile the forelegs and hindlegs extend equally with an easy reach and drive that maintains a steady topline. When moving, the head and neck should remain somewhat erect and as speed increases there is a very slight convergence of legs toward the center line. Paddling or toeing in are faults. Moving away, the hindquarters travel with moderate width between them and the foot pads can be seen. Hocks that strike each other or are thrown out to the sides are faults.

Size - Dogs and Bitches 91/2 to 11 1/2 inches should be given primary preference. Only where the comparative superiority of a specimen outside these ranges clearly justifies it, should greater latitude be taken. In no case, however, should this latitude ever extend over 12 inches or under 9 inches. The minimum limits do not apply to puppies.

Temperament - Gentle mannered, very sensitive, playful and affectionate. A cheerful attitude is the hallmark of this breed and one should settle for nothing less.

OFFICIAL STANDARD FOR THE BICHON FRISE
Approved October 11, 1988

General Appearance - The Bichon Frise is a small, sturdy, white powder puff of a dog whose merry temperament is evidenced by his plumed tail carried jauntily over the back and his dark-eyed inquisitive expression.

This is a breed that has no gross or incapacitating exaggerations, and therefore, there is no inherent reason for lack of balance or unsound movement.

Any deviation from the ideal described in the standard should be penalized to the extent of the deviation. Structural faults common to all breeds are as undesirable in the Bichon Frise as in any other breed, even though such faults may not be specifically mentioned in the standard.

Size, Proportion, Substance

Size - Dogs and bitches 9 1/2 to 11 1/2 inches are to be given primary preference. only where the comparative superiority of a specimen outside this range clearly justifies it should greater latitude be taken. In no case, however, should this latitude ever extend over 12 inches or under 9 inches. The minimum limits do not apply to puppies. *Proportion* - The body from the forward-most point of the chest to the point of rump is 1/4 longer than the height at the withers. The body from the withers to lowest point of chest represents one half the distance from withers to ground. *Substance* - Compact and of medium bone throughout; neither coarse nor fine.

Head

Expression - Soft, dark-eyed, inquisitive, alert. *Eyes* are round, black or dark brown and are set in the skull to look directly forward. An overly large or bulging eye is a fault as is an almond shaped, obliquely set eye. Halos, the black or very dark brown skin surrounding the eyes, are necessary as they accentuate the eye and enhance expression. The eye rims themselves must be black. Broken pigment, or total absence of pigment on the eye rims produce a blank and staring expression, which is a definite fault. Eyes of any color other than black or dark brown are a very serious fault and must be severely penalized. *Ears* are drop and are covered with long flowing hair. When extended toward the nose, the leathers reach approximately halfway the length of the muzzle. They are set on slightly higher than eye level and rather forward on the skull, so that when the dog is alert they serve to frame the face. The *skull* is slightly rounded, allowing for a round and forward looking eye. The *stop* is slightly accentuated. *Muzzle* - A properly balanced head is three parts muzzle to five parts skull, measured from the nose to the stop and from the stop to the occiput. A line drawn between the outside corners of the eyes and to the nose will create a near equilateral triangle. There is a slight degree of chiseling under the eyes, but not so much as to result in a weak or snipey foreface. The lower jaw is strong. The *nose* is prominent and always black. *Lips* are black, fine, never drooping. *Bite* is scissors. A bite which is undershot or overshot should be severely penalized. A crooked or out of line tooth is permissible, however, missing teeth are to be severely faulted.

Neck, Topline and Body

The arched *neck* is long and carried proudly behind an erect head. It blends smoothly into the shoulders. The length of neck from occiput to withers is approximately 1/3 the distance from forechest to buttocks. The *topline* is level except for a slight, muscular arch over the loin. *Body* - The chest is well developed and wide enough to allow free and unrestricted movement of the front legs. The lowest point of the chest extends at least to the elbow. The rib cage is moderately sprung and extends back to a short and muscular loin. The forechest is well pronounced and protrudes slightly forward of the point of shoulder. The underline has a moderate tuck-up. *Tail* is well plumed, set on level with the topline and curved gracefully over the back so that the hair of the tail rests on the back. When the tail is extended toward the head it reaches at least halfway to the withers. A low tail set, a tail carried perpendicularly to the back, or a tail which droops behind is to be severely penalized. A corkscrew tail is a very serious fault.

Forequarters

Shoulders - The shoulder blade, upper arm and forearm are approximately equal in length. The shoulders are laid back to somewhat near a forty-five-degree angle. The upper arm extends well back so the elbow is placed directly below the withers when viewed from the side. *Legs* are of medium bone; straight, with no bow or curve in the forearm or wrist. The elbows are held close to the body. The *pasterns* slope slightly from the vertical. The dewclaws may be removed. The feet are tight and round, resembling those of a cat and point directly forward, turning neither in nor out. *Pads* are black. *Nails* are kept short.

Hindquarters

The hindquarters are of medium bone, well angulated wlth muscular thighs and spaced moderately wide. The upper and lower thigh are nearly equal in length meeting at a well bent stifle joint. The leg from hock joint to foot pad is perpendicular to the ground. Dewclaws may be removed. Paws are tight and round with black pads.

Coat

The texture of the coat is of utmost importance. The undercoat is soft and dense, the outercoat of a coarser and curlier texture. The combination of the two gives a soft but substantial feel to the touch which is similar to plush or velvet and when patted springs back. When bathed and brushed, it stands off the body, creating an overall powder puff appearance. A wiry coat is not desirable. A limp, silky coat, a coat that lies down, or a lack of undercoat are very serious faults.

Trimming - The coat is trimmed to reveal the natural outline of the body. It is rounded off from any direction and never cut so short as to create an overly trimmed or squared off appearance. The furnishings of the head, beard, mustache, ears and tail are left longer. The longer head hair is trimmed to create an overall rounded in impression. The topline is trimmed to appear level. The coat is long enough to maintain the powder puff look which is characteristic of the breed.

Color

Color is white, may have shadings of buff, cream or apricot around the ears or on the body. Any color in excess of 10% of the entire coat of a mature specimen is a fault and should be penalized, but color öf the accepted shadings should not be faulted in puppies.

Gait

Movement at a trot is free, precise and effortless. In profile the forelegs and hind legs extend equally with an easy reach and drive that maintains a steady topline. When moving, the head and neck remain somewhat erect and as speed increases there is a very slight convergence of legs toward the center line. Moving away, the hindquarters travel with moderate width between them and the foot pads can be seen. Coming and going, his movement is precise and true.

Temperament

Gentle mannered, sensitive, playful and affectionate. A cheerful attitude is the hallmark of the breed and one should settle for nothing less.

PROPORTION CHART FOR THE BICHON FRISE

A-B: BODY LENGTH (sternum to buttocks) 1/4 longer than - **C-D: HEIGHT** (withers to ground). **C-E: BODY DEPTH** (withers to lowest point of chest) 1/2 of C-D (withers to ground). **E-D: LENGTH OF LEG** (elbow to ground) 1/2 of C-D (withers to ground). **C-F:** (withers to tail) 1/4 less than C-D (withers to ground). **C-G: NECK** (back of skull to withers) 1/3 length of body A-B. **H-J: HEAD** 3/8 muzzle H-I (nose to stop) and 5/8 skull I-J (stop to occiput).

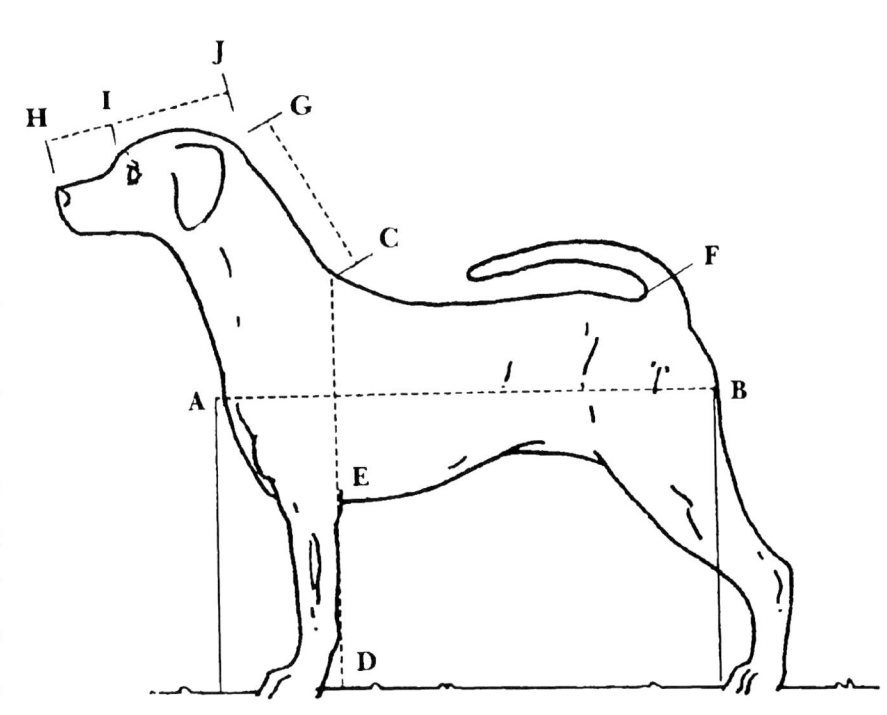

There's much about a really stylish Bichon Frise both in proportion and stance that puts the observer in mind of a little show pony. Contrast it with the dwarfed animal that appears in the foreground. The difference is as obvious as that which exists between the proper type Bichon and those that revert back to the drag of the breed.

DIFFERENCES BETWEEN THE BICHON AND THE POODLE

To illustrate the fact that a Bichon of proper proportions does not look like a Poodle, this Bichon and Poodle are drawn at exactly the same height, only their proportions are different. The Bichon Standard calls for a body (A-B) that is at most 1/4 longer than the dog's height at the shoulder (C-D). This makes the length of back (C-E) approximately 1/4 shorter than the dog's height at the shoulder.

The Poodle Standard calls for a body (A-B) that squares with the dog's height at the shoulder (C-D). This makes the back (C-E) significantly shorter than that called for in the Bichon Standard. It should be easy to see that if in fact a Bichon is constructed according to the breed standard there is little resemblance to the Poodle's extremes nor would the Bichon be long or low.

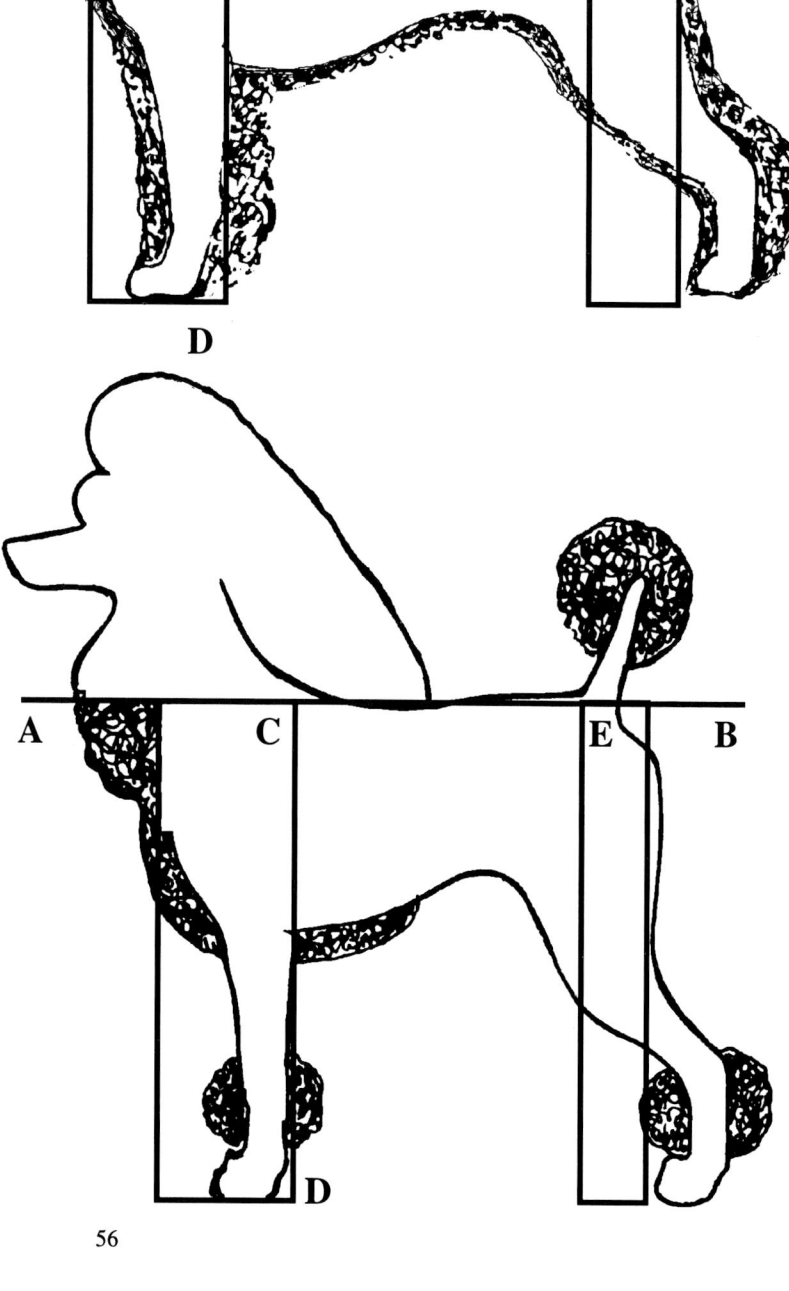

Proper balance of height to length, leg to body and proper length of neck combine to give the breed the glamorous look it has been associated with as demonstrated by the dog in the photograph above.

Although this Bichon (left) has a very pleasing head, good pigment and an apparently excellent quality coat, his short legs completely destroy balance and diminish the elegant look the breed is capable of.

Checking under the coat of the short legged dog will reveal the length of forearm does not equal the distance from highest point of withers to bottom of chest.

The properly proportioned dog appears well balanced and proportionate even without the benefit of its luxurious coat.

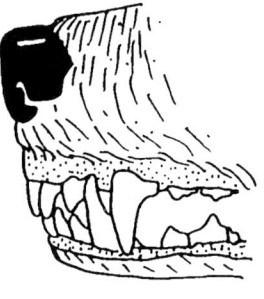

The Bichon Frise standard calls for a scissors bite. Pictured here also are the overshot and the undershot bites.

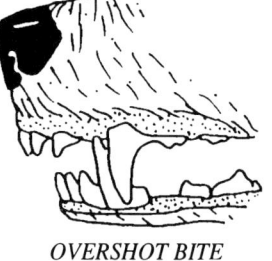

CORRECT BITE

OVERSHOT BITE

UNDERSHOT BITE

In order to achieve the right expression the Bichon's skull must have sufficient width and curvature to allow room for its large, well spaced and forward looking eyes. There is enough strength to the muzzle to accomodate the large black nose. Strength of under jaw helps give a look of strength to the muzzle.

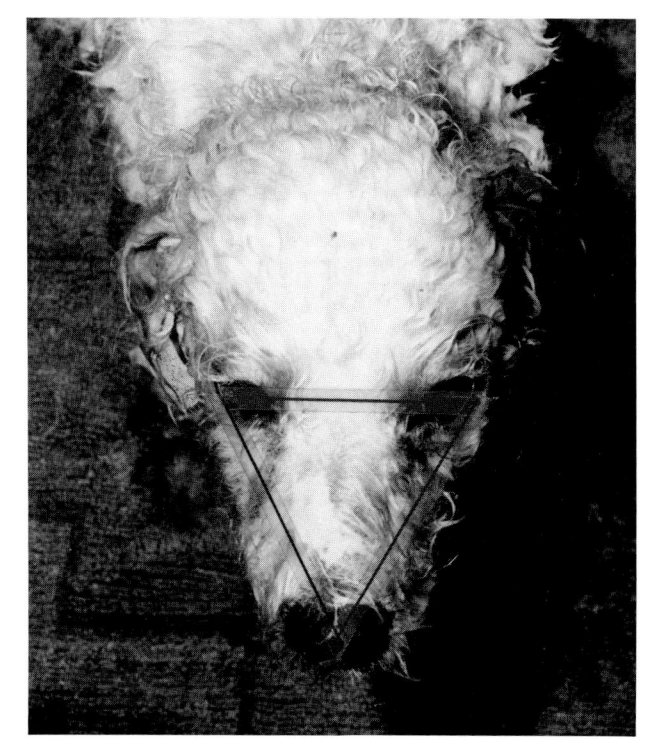

Looking down on the head a line drawn to the outside corners of the eyes and to the end of the nose creates an aquilateral triangle. It should be evident that this can only be accomplished with proper width of skull and the correct muzzle/skull proportions.

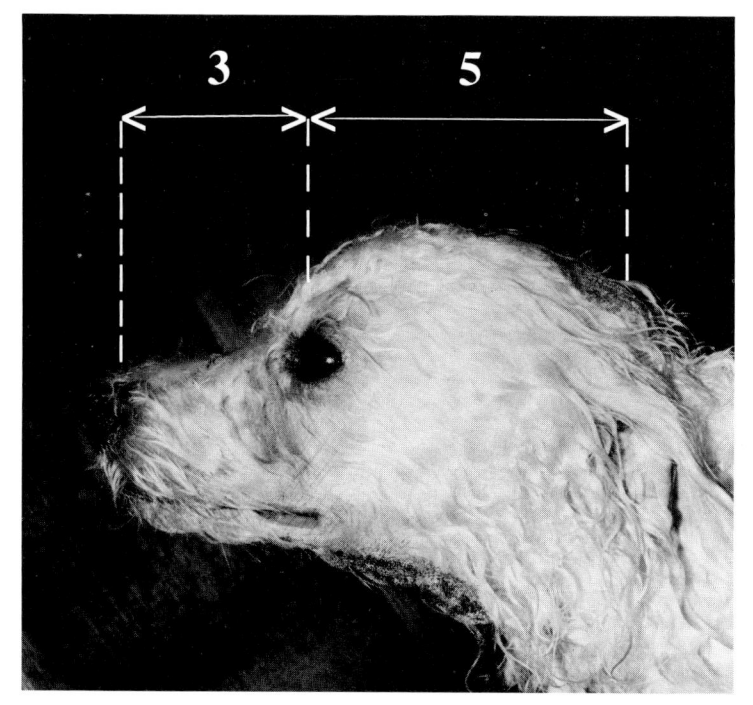

In profile the Bichon's muzzle to skull proportions are as 3 is to 5. Longer muzzles give an extremely foreign and down-faced look. The shorter muzzle lends itself to an oriental look and is often accompanied by an undershot bite.

58

EXPRESSION... HEAD ON

This male's head proportions and jet black pigmentation create the ideal Bichon expression.

Although this youngster does not yet have adult coat, she could never be mistaken for any other breed nor could she be anything other than female.

Another male who exhibits all the necessary elements that go into creating the unique Bichon head piece and expression.

No long explanation should be necessary to illustrate why the Bichon syandard calls for good length of neck. Imagine, if you will, what a major difference correct length of neck would make on the dog pictured on the left.

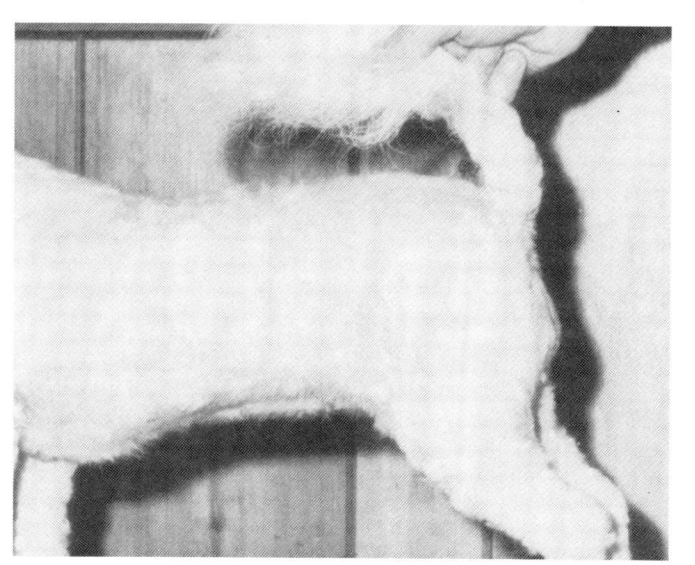

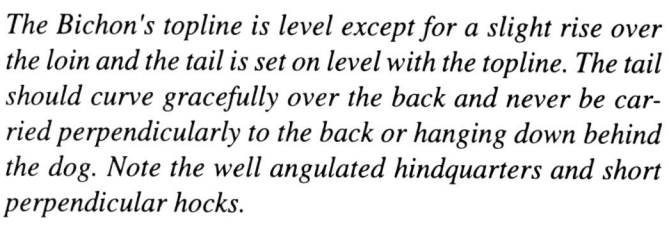

The Bichon's topline is level except for a slight rise over the loin and the tail is set on level with the topline. The tail should curve gracefully over the back and never be carried perpendicularly to the back or hanging down behind the dog. Note the well angulated hindquarters and short perpendicular hocks.

The straight forward movement of the forequarters is assisted by a well-developed chest that extends to the elbow. This construction helps to stabilize and firmly anchor the front legs. It is important to remember that the Bichon has a prominent sternum and well developed rib cage. The rib cage itself is long and is how proper body length is achieved. The Bichon does NOT achieve its body length through a long loin and/or a long back. (Please refer to pages 74-75 for additional discussion of front and shoulder construction.)

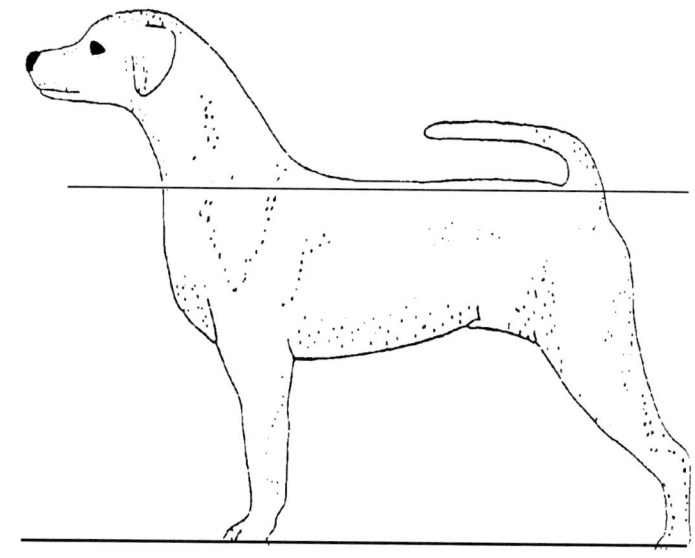

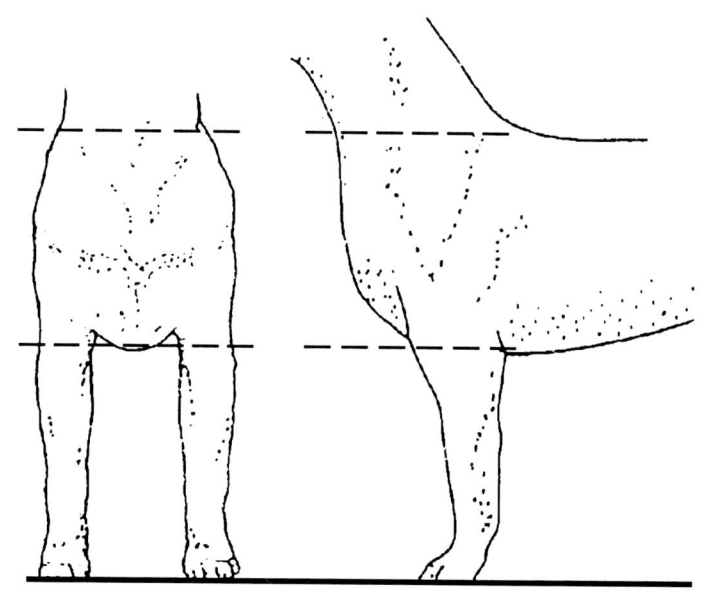

Hindquarters should be muscular, of medium bone and nicely angulated. The upper and lower thigh are nearly equal in length meeting at a well bent stifle joint.

The straight rearquarter elevates the rear end of the Bichon and restricts the drive and follow through which are so important and typical to the breed's profile movement.

The standard is very specific in asking the coat to be trimmed to follow the natural outline of the dog. Exaggerations of any kind are to be discouraged (i.e. carrying the neck line all the way down to the middle of the back, chopping the ear fringe so short as to give the breed a "prick-eared" look, etc.). The young class dog or bitch will not carry the amount or density of coat of the mature Specials dog but still it can be trimmed properly and promise the finished texture.

The Specials dog on the other hand will have a wealth of coat of firm-but-not-coarse texture. This does not mean, however, that "more is better." Properly trimmed, the Bichon coat should never interfere with full view of all four of the legs in movement. The Bichon's profile movement is a hallmark of the breed and should never be obscured. Note the natural look of this dog's head trim. It permits the natural fall of the ears without giving the dog an unattractive top-heavy look.

This classic photo of the Chaminade Five shows the dogs with lovely, natural head trims - rounded but not fashioned to look like a West Highland White Terrier. It should be remembered that the standard asks for a soft, natural look and is specific in discouraging exaggerations. In the inset (left) this dog's extreme head trim resembles the faddish exaggeration unfortunately becoming popularized both here and abroad.

Look for the Bichon that moves freely and easily around the ring with steady reach and drive. Those dogs lacking in front reach and rear follow-through are to be penalized accordingly. In watching rearquarter movement it is important that the rear pastern between hock and foot must extend rearward well beyond the vertical. Simply observing the dog's black pads while it moves away does not actually indicate sufficient follow through in the rear. Follow through is best observed in profile.

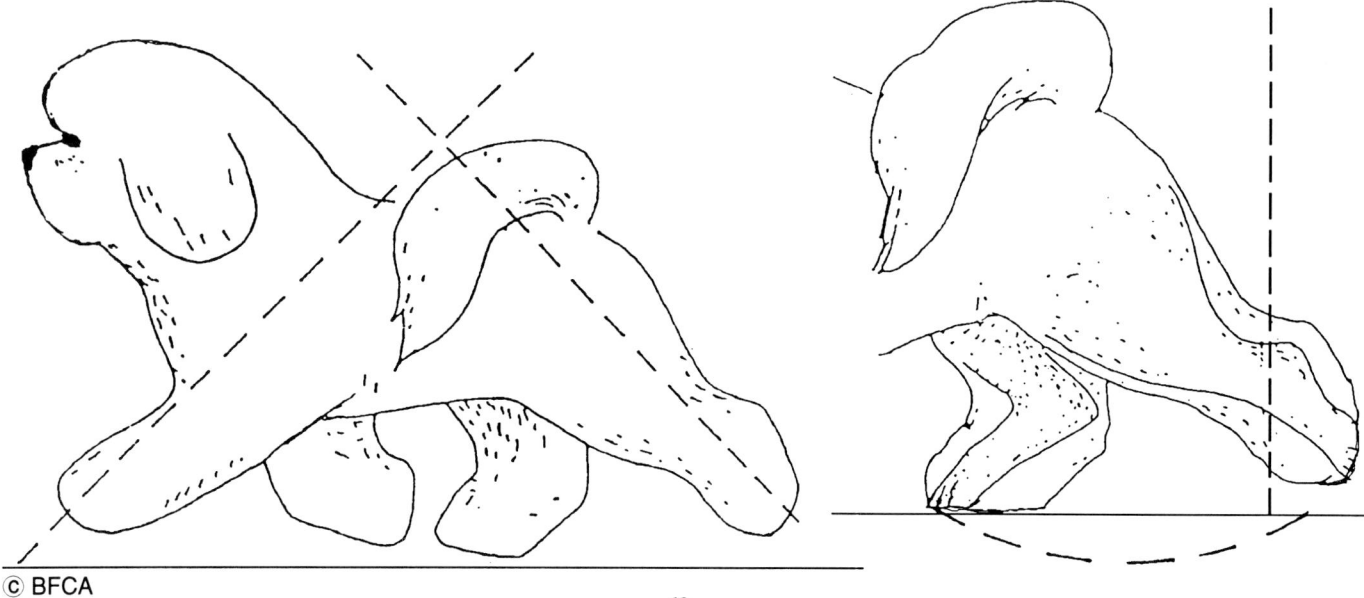

© BFCA

BUILT RIGHT
TO
MOVE RIGHT
&
STAND RIGHT

Correct movement is not limited to any dog within the desired size range. Whether 9 and a half or 11 and a half inches, the properly constructed Bichon can and should move with reach and drive. Pictured (above) Hicker Ain't I Smart (England), then (left) Ch. Camelot's Brassy Nickel (Eastern U.S.) and (lower right) Ch. Chaminade Le Jazz Hot (West Coast U.S.) reveal neither size, pedigree nor part of the world limit a breeder's ability to produce correct movement. In the end there is nothing that tells more about how well a Bichon is constructed than how it looks standing on its own in the ring. Temperament, balance, maneuverability are all clearly and easily revealed.

SEEN RINGSIDE

On the right, Dakota's loyal fans, Sandon's Whispered Gossip and "Gremlin" owned by Chris Henkel & Mary Ann Larssen. Photo by Ric

Joe Waterman with Ch. Vogelflight's Music Man and Tim Brazier with Ch. Rimskittle Bartered Bride go Two and One in the group at the Long Beach KC in the 1970's. Photo by Ludwig

Chapter III
PRODUCING PATTERNS
The First Two Decades

ALL TIME TOP PRODUCING SIRES

1.	**Ch. Chaminade Mr. Beau Monde**	65
	(Ch. Cali-Col's Robspierre ex Ch. Reenroy's Ami du Kilkanney)	
2.	**Ch. Vogelflight's Music Man**	47
	(Ch. Chaminade Mr. Beau Monde ex Ch. Vogelflight Diandee Amy Pouf)	
3.	**Ch. Teeny Tepees Chief of Diandee**	38
	(Ch. Reenroy's Royal Flush de Noel ex Teeny Tepee's Mauri Juleene)	
4.	**Ch. Beau Monde the Huckster**	35
	(Ch. Teeny Tepees Chief of Diandee ex Ch. Beau Monde the Stripper)	
5.	**Ch. Leander Snow Star**	34
	(Leander Snow Venture ex Ch. C & D Beau Monde Sunflower)	
6.	**Ch. C & D Count Kristopher**	29
	(Peppe de Barnette ex Quentia of Goldysdale)	
7.	**Ch. Diamonts Le Magnifique**	27
	(Ch. Ardezz Jacque's Diament ex Ch. Diament's Dominique)	
	Ch. Loftiss Reenie	27
	(Reenroy's Toro ex Reenroy Tanya)	
8.	**Ch. Dove Cote's Mr. Magoo**	26
	(Ch. Whitegold Razzberry Jubilee ex Ch. Dove Cote's Emily Doggenson)	
	Ch. Parfait Coming Home	26
	(Ch. L'Havre Joyeux Desi ex Ch. Parfait Apple Crunch)	
9.	**Ch. Montravia Jazz M'Tazz**	25
	(Leijazulip Jazz of Zudiki ex Montravia Snow Dream)	
	Ch. Paw Mark's Talk of the Town	25
	(Ch. Jalwin Just A Jiffy ex Ch. Tres Beau Impeccable Imp)	
	Ch. Sandon's Friendly Legacy	25
	(Ch. Sandon's Friend ex Ch. WinMars Lucy Lucille)	
10.	**Ch. Jalwin Just A Jiffy**	22
	(Ch. Diandee Masterpiece ex Ch. Jalwin Panache of WinMar)	
	Ch. Sumarco Alaafee Top Gun	22
	(Ch. Montravia Jazz M'Tazz ex Paper Lace of Zudiki)	

ALL TIME TOP PRODUCING DAMS

1.	Ch. Beau Monde The Firecracker	17	9.	Ch. Ardezz Juliette Diamont	8
2.	Ch. C and D's Countess Becky	16		Ch. Beau Monde Works D'Arte Witty	8
3.	Ch. Jalwin Panache of WinMar	14		Ch. Bella Graziella of Dejavu	8
4.	Ch. Deja Vu Touch of Scandal	13		Ch. Bunnyrun Over the Rainbow	8
	Ch. Vogelflight's Fantasia	13		Ch. C and D's Sunbonnet	8
5.	Ch. Dove Cote's Poise N Ivory	12		EE's R Royale Trinquette	8
6.	Ch. Norvic's Alpine Sparkler	11		Ch. Gabby's Angel of Willow Wink	8
7.	Ch. Balverne Fleur Lalique	10		Ch. Jalwin Justice	8
	Ch. Baebra Gatlock of Druid	10		Ch. Kobold's Eleusinian Mystery	8
	Braymar's Bali-Hai	10		Ch. Tanya	8
	Ch. Paw Mark Popin Fresh Tres Beau	10	10.	Ch. Belinda De Windstar	7
	Ch. Parfait Ebony and Ivory	10		Ch. Chaminade Bleu Velvet	7
	Ch. Sha-Bob's Nice Girl Missy	10		Ch. Foxlaur's Bette Lu of Druid	7
	Ch. Tomaura's Touch of Elegance	10		Ch. Glen Elfred's Misty Blu	7
8.	Ch. C and D's Beau Monde Moonshine	9		Ch. Les Mieux's Regal Victoria	7
	Ch. Cali-Col's Shalimar of Reenroy	9		Ch. Mel Mar Chou Chou de Noel	7
	Ch. Diamant's Dominique	9		Ch. Norvic's Elaquance	7
	Ch. Ladywoods Chi Chi Beene	9		Ch. Paw Marks Lollipop Labow	7
	Ch. Miri Cals Arabella	9		Ch. Rank's Tar Baby of Lejerdell	7
	Ch. Reenroy's Image of Ami	9		Ch. Sandcastle Bikini	7
	Ch. Sandcastle Gold Coast Dixie	9		Ch. Sheramor Showtime Lady	7
				Ch. Tomaura's Amber De Susa	7
				Ch. Win-Mar's Lucy Lucille	7
				Ch. Win-Mar's Three Coins of Druid	7
				Woodway Wynn De Baudier	7

Statistics based on all AKC championships confirmed and corrected for 1973, the first year of recorded championships through the close of the 1995 producing year. Statistics compiled by Anne D. Hearn.

Although Ch. C & D Countess Becky's granddaughter, Ch. Beau Monde The Firecracker produced one more champion (17) than Becky (right), there is no doubt whatsoever that Becky stands as one of the most influential bitches in the history of the breed. She, along with Ch. Reenroy's Ami du Kilkanny can rightfully take their place as the two most important bitches in the history of the breed in America.

Ch. Beau Monde The Firecracker is Winners Bitch, Best Opposite Sex at Somerset Hills KC in 1973. Photo by Ashbey.

ALL TIME TOP PRODUCING BREEDERS

#	Name	Count	#	Name	Count
1.	Dolores Wolske	128	14.	Judith Hilmer	38
2.	Barbara Stubbs	73		Betsy Schley	38
3.	Richard Beauchamp	71		Norman Vicha	38
4.	Betty Keatley	70	15.	Charles Wolske	37
5.	Sharan Fry	65	16.	Clover Allen	36
6.	Laura Purnell	61		Beth Jones	36
7.	Karla Matlock	56		Jane Lagemann	36
	Pauline Schultz	56		Les Matlock	36
8.	Alice Vicha	55		Jean Rank	36
9.	Gertrude Fournier	45	17.	Lorrie Carlton-Conrad	35
10.	Mayree Butler	44		Doris Hyde	35
11.	Eleanor Grassick	43		Ginger LeCave	35
12.	Miriam Barnhart	41	18.	Judy Fausset	33
	Lois Morrow	41		Gene Mills	33
13.	Margaret Britton	39	19.	Joanne Spilman	32
	Judith Thayer	39	20.	Mary Ellen Mills	31

Ch. Chaminade Le Blanc Chamour "Beemer" contemplates some of his awards.

PEDIGREE OF CH. CHAMINADE MR. BEAU MONDE

Mr. Beau Monde is the breed's top producing sire of all time with 65 AKC champions to his credit. There is no record of his many other champions in countries throughout the world. "Christopher" sired his first champion when he was 12 months old and his last two champions were sired when he was 14, just 6 months before he died.

		Jou Jou De Hoop
	Andre De Gascoigne	
		Hermine De Hoop
Mex.Ch. Dapper Dan de Gascoigne		
		Amigo-Mio D'Egriselles
	Lady Des Frimoussettes	
		Houpette Des Frimoussettes
Ch. Cali-Col Robspierre		
		Youbi
	Helly of Milton	
		Zoee of Milton
Lyne of Milton		
		Youbi
	Hanette of Milton	
		Zoee of Milton
CH. CHAMINADE MR. BEAU MONDE		
		Jou Jou De Hoop
	Andre De Gascoigne	
		Hermine De Hoop
Mex.Ch. Dapper Dan de Gascoigne		
		Amigo-Mio D'Egriselles
	Lady Des Frimoussettes	
		Houpette Des Frimoussettes
CH. Reenroy's Ami du Kilkanny		
		Int.Ch. Bandit de Steren Vor
	Eddy White De Steren Vor	
		Ami Du Lary
Little Nell of Cali-Col		
		Eddy White De Steren Vor
	Nelly of Cali-Col	
		Lassy of Milton

PEDIGREE OF CH. BEAU MONDE THE FIRECRACKER

The Firecracker, heavily bred on the French, Ombre de la Roche Posay line. She proved to be an excellent nick with descendants of the Belgian lines. She was the dam of 17 champions.

		Int.Ch. JimboJ de Steren Vor
	Quintal de Warnabry	
		Int.Ch. Janitzia de Steren Vor
Peppe de Barnette		
		Int.Ch. Jimbo de Steren Vor
	Romance de Bourbiel	
		Int.Ch. Kitoune de Steren Vor
Ch. C and D's Count Kristopher		
		Izor Prince des Frimoussettes
	Ombre de la Roche Posay	
		Iona II de la Roche Posay
Quentia of Goldysdale		
		Izor Prince des Frimoussettes
	Oree de la Roche Posay	
		Forne de Dierstein
CH. BEAU MONDE THE FIRECRACKER		
		Dapper Dan de Gascoigne
	Ch. Cali-Col's Robspierre	
		Lyne of Milton
Ch. Chaminade Mr. Beau Monde		
		Dapper Dan de Gascoigne
	Ch. Reenroy's Ami du Kilkanny	
		Little Nell of Cali-Col
Ch. C and D Beau Monde Sunbeam		
		Quintal de Warnabry
	Peppe de Barnette	
		Romance de Bourbiel
Ch. C and D's Countess Becky		
		Ombre de la Roche Posay
	Quentia of Goldysdela	
		Oree de la Roche Posay

Chapter IV
INTERPRETING THE STANDARD

1988 Standard Clarification

The 1988 Breed Standard Revision Committee of the Bichon Frise Club of America invested considerable effort to say nothing of time in responding to the AKC's request that breed parent clubs reformat their standards. The AKC had no intention of changing standards, only to create some consistency as to where specific information could be found within the various standards. For example, all standards would begin with "General Appearance" and this would be followed by "Size, proportion and substance."

The BFCA, however, took this opportunity to deal with the anatomical questions that had hitherto been ignored or avoided for reasons described earlier in the history chapter of this book. It was time to eliminate confusion by defining proportions once and for all and by substantiating those definitions with information contained in the original French Standard of the breed.

Although it was to take many drafts, the Committee concluded their work with a standard that clearly defined what the breed was and had always been intended to be. The final draft was submitted to the entire membership and though there were undoubtedly individuals throughout the breed whose personal agendas had not been entirely fulfilled, still the new standard was approved by an overwhelming majority as required by the Constitution of the Bichon Frise Club of America, Inc.

The standard clarification reduced the ambiguities that the previous standard had contained to an absolute minimum. The standard as approved by the AKC in October of 1988 gave both breeder and judge an ideal with which to compare any specimen of the breed. It was no longer a question of individual preference but of what was actually required.

Breed Type and "Style"

It should be understood that there are always interpretations of the standard that are capable of creating a slightly different picture from breeder to breeder. However, there is only one standard and one correct type. I wrote about this at great length as part of a series for *Dogs In Canada*. The piece was very well received and, in fact was responsible for winning the Dog Writer's Association of America's 1996 Award for Best Subject Related Series.

In the article I made reference to a column written by Susan B. Lennard, the St. Bernard columnist for the *American Kennel Club Gazette: Purebred Dogs*. Ms. Lennard's article helps considerably in understanding what often takes place in regard to correct type and its interpretation. She refers to the standard of her breed as "the definitive description of breed type" and a breeder's *expression* of that ideal as "style." She writes, "The extent of that expression may contribute to or deviate from aspects of the phenotype described in our standard." She then goes on to say, "Style may be an adjunct to type, but it is not the same thing."

I have no argument with those who subscribe to the theory that there are many expressions of that single ideal which we all pursue. However, I find it impossible to accept the premise that just any and all expressions of type are equally valid.

There always has been, and hopefully will always be, room for argument as to just how close even the best of our outstanding dogs approach the ideal. However, I seldom find knowledgeable individuals who do not agree that our best have at least earned a permanent place of distinction. There can be little argument that Mrs. William Tabler's Ch. Chaminade Syncopation was as correct for his day as we were able to understand. Nor can anyone refute the great good he did as a show dog. That he did not look much like Nancy Shapland's Devon Puff And Stuff is of little consequence. Puff represented the advances we had made in the time that had lapsed between Syncopation and Puff's meteoric career.

As I wrote for my piece in *Dogs In Canada*, "Beauty does indeed have its own hierarchy. The ability to see it and an uncompromising desire to reproduce it are absolute conditions for success."

Discussing the Standard

GENERAL APPEARANCE

In 1988 as part of the AKC's standardization process they requested that all references to other animals in the standards of the breeds be removed. Therefore, those involved in drafting the 1988 standard clarification were unable to include several short lines that have helped define the character and general appearance of Bichon Frise so well over the years. The reference is one that should be committed to memory as it sums up what we hope to see in the show quality Bichon. It appeared originally in *The Bichon Frise Today* which was published in 1982. It read as follows:

"There is a great deal about the correct Bichon Frise that will remind one of the little show pony. Both stand over their fronts, arch their necks and thrust their rear quarters out behind them. Their attitudes are jaunty and cocky, yet there is something elegant in their stance."

Were we unable to say anything else about the breed, these few lines create a vivid image of the ideal Bichon standing still. The picture denotes angulation as well and it is the beautifully angulated front and corresponding rear that give the Bichon its distinctive and free flowing reach and drive. Watching the Bichon's profile movement tells you much about how the dog is put together.

In 1974 Tom Stevenson spoke before a Judges Education Seminar and spoke of the Bichon whose "(current) American standard had not quite kept up with the progress of the breed." His vivid description of the Bichon captured the very essence of the breed then and it holds to this day.

"It's a white powder-puff of a dog to look at, and a substantial dog to feel. It's a compact dog, made more so by a coat that is rounded off from any direction. It gives you balance, it gives you expression. Just be sure you've got bone and substance in balance, a forechest, a rib cage carried back to a short loin and the ninety degree angulation to permit the kind of movement the standard doesn't tell you about. That movement is the family hallmark passed on to the derivative breeds, a delight in profile, with steady

Photo by Missy

The "Lady in Black," Barbara Stubbs and son, Bruce in 1972 with a wagon load of Chaminade Bichons. Photo by Missy.

topline and pads they show you from the rear."

I find it particularly interesting that Stevenson's comments, although they came from someone outside of the breed, reflected exactly what those of us within the breed were hoping to see become the norm for the breed. And further, that his comments gave, albeit in a more visually descriptive manner, exactly that which the French standard intended to convey in 1933.

The striking contrast of jet black pigmentation against a snowy white background of course help complete the breed's exquisite picture. Although the current standard does not waste the reader's time by listing every conceivable fault that might occur in the breed, anything that detracts from the picture described or is a fault interfering with soundness and movement should be considered and penalized to the extent to which it does interfere with what has been asked for.

SIZE, PROPORTION AND SUBSTANCE

Size: The standard includes a very wide size range (9 1/2 to 11 1/2 inches) and there should be no prejudice given for or against any Bichon that falls within that size range. The emphasis in evaluating the Bichon should be placed on how much quality the individual has, not where it falls within the size range. Since the size range remains the same for both dog and bitch it is conceivable that one's best male could be at the bottom of the scale while the best bitch might approach the top limits.

At the same time it should be understood that the specimen too large (over the permitted size range) or the individual that falls below the size perimeter is not typical and should be given little consideration, if any for the winner's circle.

Proportion: Correct proportions give the Bichon Frise the silhouette by which it is recognized. Proportions are a significant part of what separates it from its two close cousins, the Havanese and the Bolognese and also what separate it from its more distant relatives the Maltese and the Poodle.

Coat and scissors do not create the correct proportions, proper construction does. Clever scissors can produce a deceiving silhouette but the breeder and the judge must not be fooled by a well done coiffure.

The Bichon's conformation is beautifully balanced and proportioned and when correct does not give one the look of a Poodle nor should there be any hint of a short-legged low slung animal. The latter is the drag of the breed and if the observer is forced to make a decision between the dog leaning toward more leg than it should have and one that leans toward insufficient leg, the strongest penalty should be levied against the short-legged dog. It is the latter that breeders are most apt to find the most difficult fault to eradicate from their breeding programs. Short legs are the drag of the breed and thus constitute an extremely serious fault. Understand, however, that the longer legged dog is not *preferred*, only that it is the lesser of two faults.

Substance: It is not unusual to find the dog that stands too high on leg is also too fine of bone while the short legged dog is inclined toward the massive bone found in many dwarfed breed. Neither is correct. The ideal Bichon has medium bone in keeping with its size.

HEAD

Expression: Measure as much as one might if the results of those measurements do not reveal the sparkling, alert nature of the Bichon Frise, they are of no consequence. Cheerfulness is the hallmark of the Bichon Frise and if the expression revealing that attitude is not there, measurements mean nothing

Eyes: The eyes are dark—sparkling. Often described as the snow man's lumps of coal set in a snowy cloud of white. The eyes are surrounded by the black pigment called "halos." The combination of the two make the Bichon's eyes a prominent feature but this is not to be misconstrued to mean protruding by any means. The bulging eye gives the breed a startled, rather than cheerful and inquisitive look. The correct eyes are set to look directly forward and one is apt to find the obliquely set eye is inclined to take on an almond shape. This configuration of the eye very often indicates a narrow skull.

Proper pigmentation is of great consequence. The eye rims themselves must be black and broken pigment indicates a degeneration of that important aspect of the breed.

Ears: The Bichon is a drop eared breed. Grooming style has all but obliterated this fact and made it appear almost to be a prick-eared breed which is not the case. Long time breeder Mary Vogel of Vogelflight fame is most emphatic in her concern over the change which has occurred in that respect. She says, "...over the years the pattern has become tighter and the head trim has gone from an elongated bell to a shorter version, however, the totally round West Highland Terrier look is incorrect. The Bichon has a drop ear, not a prick ear. Why try to make it appear otherwise? This (the correct ear) is very important for the true Bichon expression."

MUZZLE AND SKULL

Skull: A properly balanced head is three parts muzzle (nose to stop) to five parts skull (stop to occiput). Looking down on the head a line drawn from the outside corners of the eyes to the end of the nose creates what is basically an equilateral triangle. There must be enough width and curvature of the skull to accommodate the forward looking eye and give room for sufficient space between the eyes. Close set eyes result in a an extremely foreign look.

Muzzle: Muzzle strength is as important to the expression as it is to proper detention. Adequate attention must be given to proper length of muzzle. A long muzzle gives a downface look. The black pigment on the lips of a strong under jaw underlines the nose and adds to the jaunty expression of the breed. A receding under jaw not only produces a weak look it somehow results in a loss of that vital and intelligent expression so important to the breed.

Lips: Spotted or entirely pink areas on the lips indicate a weakness of pigment and strong pigmentation is obviously of utmost importance in the Bichon. Drooping flews would tend to reveal the pink gums of the mouth which again would detract from the black-on-white contrast so highly desirable.

Bite: Both the undershot and overshot jaws are extremely objectionable in the Bichon. No mention is made of the level bite in the standard which leaves much to the discretion of the observer. While level bites are certainly not be encouraged in any way, still they must be dealt with within the context of degree. Personally I feel this is far less grievous a fault if the jaws themselves are properly aligned and it is only the teeth meeting in a level bite. But there again, some individuals see the entire dog hanging from its teeth.

NECK, TOPLINE AND BODY

Neck: The elegantly arched neck is a prominent feature of the Bichon. Ideally, it is one third of the length of the body (from sternum to buttocks) and begins its arch at the occiput blending into the well laid back shoulders. It carries the head proudly and gracefully.

Topline: The topline as described in the standard refers only to the area from the top of the shoulders to the set on of tail. However, it is difficult to separate the long, arched neck from the picture that creates the topline. Starting at the occiput we see a long graceful curve into the shoulders where the line straightens out except for an almost imperceptible rise over the loin.

Body: The rise over the loin in the Bichon Frise is created by both muscle and height of the rib vertebrae spires. The additional strength provided by this construction contributes to the agility and maneuverability in the rear quarter. It is important to understand that the "rise" as described in the standard not be confused with what is commonly known as a "high rear" or "reverse topline." The latter are faults created by short upper arms in the forehand and a straight, long-boned rear quarter that pitches the rear end

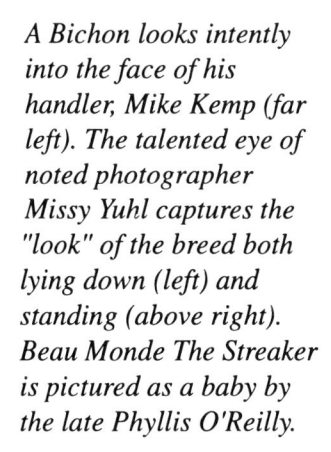

A Bichon looks intently into the face of his handler, Mike Kemp (far left). The talented eye of noted photographer Missy Yuhl captures the "look" of the breed both lying down (left) and standing (above right). Beau Monde The Streaker is pictured as a baby by the late Phyllis O'Reilly.

well above the front end. If the current standard is lacking in any respect it is in its neglecting to place sufficient emphasis on the need for a prominent fore chest and sternum in the breed. Lacking in this respect, the breed tends toward raciness, lacking in rib spring and substance throughout. Further, it adversely affects overall proportions.

If the Bichon's proper additional length of body over height is to come from the area forechest to buttocks and we have little or no fore chest, we have seriously shortened body length. Were this shortcoming adjusted by additional length of the ribcage it would not be quite so serious a fault. More often than not, however, the extra length is compensated for by a short ribcage and additional length in the loin area. In so doing we are creating a weakness in the area that permits the spring and maneuverability so important to the breed.

Tail: The high set on of the tail allows the Bichon to carry its tail over the back effortlessly. When the dog is at rest the tail will lie on the back. The low set tail creates any number of problems.

Photo by Lawrence.

The low set tail is the result of a croup that slopes downward to a marked degree turning the entire rearquarter under the dog. At rest the tail then unfurls and hangs down behind the dog. Even more important than the dismal picture this creates is that this construction severely limits the rearward extension of the hindquarter in movement—the dog moves "under" itself.

There are few breeds whose outline is changed as drastically by improper tail carriage as is the Bichon. It drastically alters outline and is certainly does nothing to create an image of a cheerful outgoing companion dog so specifically described in the breed standard.

FOREQUARTERS

Breeders and judges write about front ends, talk about them, even cry about them but the problem remains the same. From the Sporting Group on through to the Herding Group, if you are going to find a common problem in show dogs, you'll find it up front. The difficulty begins at the top of the shoulder blade, runs down through it to the upper arm, continues on into the forearm, the pastern and stops at the feet (I guess because there is no place for the problem to move on to!).

Because front end construction does include such a myriad of complex problem areas the potential for something to go wrong is monumental. And, contrary to what far too many people want to think, changing one bone immediately affects what happens to those attached to it. The old Negro spiritual song, "Dem Bones, Dem Bones" has application that reaches far outside the doors of a church!

If one wants to fully understand how the properly made Bichon gets its "look" and how it moves in the manner it does, a full understanding of the front end construction is mandatory.

Shoulders: the shoulder blade, upper arm and

forearm should be approximately equal in length. The shoulders are laid back to somewhat near a forty-five degree angle. The upper arm extends well back so that the elbow is placed directly below the withers when viewed from the side.

DISCUSSION: As previously discussed one is most apt to find a good pair of shoulders on a dog that has correct length of neck and long rib cage. The three support each other and those three portions of the anatomy constitute the major portion of the front assembly.

The angulation of the shoulder blade (scapula), upper arm (humerus) and forearm (radius ulna) required by the standard is to provide maximum reach with the least effort. This is illustrated above. The principle governing reach becomes obvious when we take a closer look at the point of connection between the scapula and the humerus. The scapula has a socket with a nose thrust forward on it. The humerus has a bald head hooked to the top side with a knob that, as the joint opened, strikes the nose of the shoulder blade socket and stops its movement in that direction. At the very best, a dog will not step beyond the point where a line drawn down the center of the scapula when stationary, intersects the ground.

When the dog is standing in a natural, stationary position, you can locate the center line of the blade by the ridge which runs down through its center. Project this line to the ground and the foot pad will not extend beyond that point when the dog moves.

Compare the well-laid-back shoulder with the straight shoulder of 60 degrees below. You can easily see how much more reach a dog is capable of with a correct shoulder than he is with a straight shoulder.

Legs: should be of medium bone not too fine or too coarse, straight with no bow or curve in the forearm or wrist. The elbows are held close to the body.

DISCUSSION: Straightforward movement depends upon straight forequarters held in place with proper shoulders and width of chest. The coat can be deceiving so it is wise to check both forelegs carefully. In Bichons it is not unusual to find only one bowed foreleg.

Pasterns: slope slightly from the vertical.

DISCUSSION: One should not confuse crooked pasterns which are viewed from the front, with slightly oblique pasterns which are viewed from the side.

Moderately sloping pasterns are associated with good construction and movement in that they are part of the bone assembly which receive and cushion im-

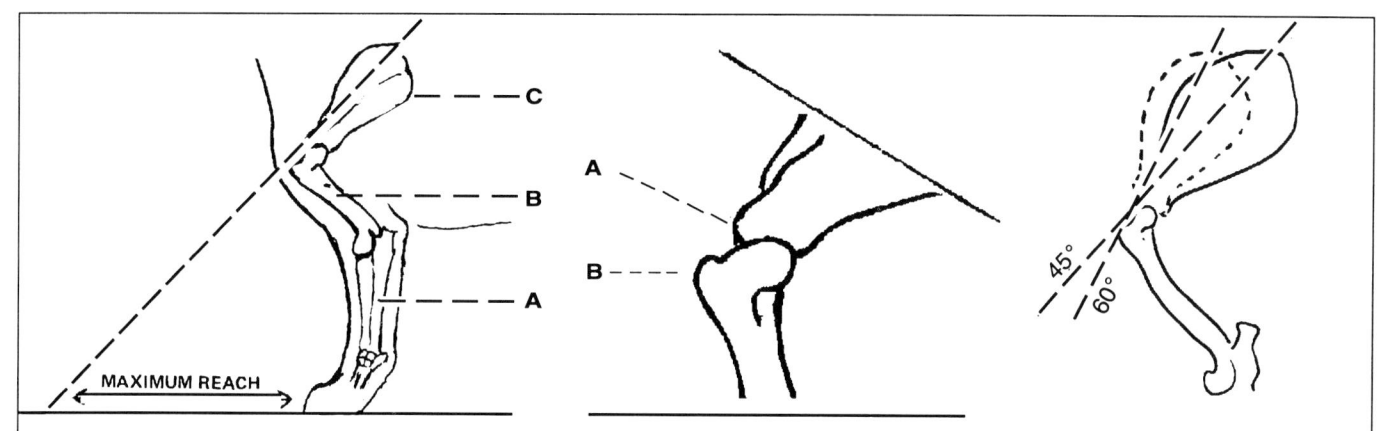

The Shoulder blade (scapula - C), upper arm (humerus - B) and forearm (radius and ulna - A) in profile. The second illustration provides a closer view of the connection between the shoulder blade (A) and the upper arm (B). The third illustration shows the difference in reach allowed by a 60 degree and a 45 degree shoulder angle. It must be remembered that 45 degrees is theoretically considered the "ideal" and is seldom if ever achieved in nature.

pact from the ground. A pastern with slight bend has spring and resilience. Straight or steep pasterns take impact with the ground head-on, jarring the entire front assembly of the dog.

Watch a good moving dog going round the ring, noting that his shoulders and topline barely rise and fall as he circles the ring. Sloping pasterns help cushion the impact which would otherwise be received by the shoulder. A dog with straight pasterns will come slamming down on his front and you'll be able to see the jarring result as his shoulders rise and fall with each stride.

Feet: The Bichon's foot is compact and round. It is what one would expect from an agile dog.

Pads: The feet are another point at which strength of pigmentation can be assessed. Just as a pink spotted nose or lips indicate a degeneration of pigmentation, so do pink foot pads.

Nails: Long nails can cause discomfort and impede good movement. Anything that impedes the Bichon's ability to move freely and quickly must be considered a fault and many a good front has been ruined through neglect.

HINDQUARTERS

DISCUSSION: Since we have determined that a well laid back shoulder permits maximum reach, it stands to reason that the Bichon must have a rearquarter that provides matching drive from behind.

The well angulated hindquarter permits the Bichon to both reach forward under his body and to extend his leg out well behind (follow through) resulting in what is referred to as "drive" behind. It also produces a very "finished" picture to the Bichon silhouette. Cowhocks are a fault underlining the standard's demand for proper movement. The term "cowhocks" was derived from the rear stance of a cow which allows room for oversized udders. Any book on dog anatomy will agree that cowhocks are a deterrent to drive from behind in that rather than permitting forward thrust, the efficiency of the rear leg is reduced since the thrust is at an angle to the line of motion.

COAT

Texture: The desired coat type is at best extremely difficult to describe or, for that matter, to picture effectively. Yet, the coat itself is most impostant to the appearance of the Bichon.

The Bichon has a double coat. A double coat is defined in *"The Complete Dog Book, The American Kennel Club"* as follows:

"An outer coat resistant to weather and protective against brush and brambles, together with an undercoat of softer hair for warmth and waterproofing."

This double coat immediately sets the Bichon apart from anything even remotely resembling the straight Maltese coat. On the other hand, the Bichon's coat is not the wirey, stiff and coarse hair of the Standard Poodle. When the standard states, "A silky coat is a fault" it means to emphasize that the Maltese type coat is incorrect for the Bichon but does not mean that the hair is not soft to the touch.

Ch. Devon Puff and Stuff　　　　*Photo by Ashbey.*

Trimming: The properly trimmed Bichon coat must give the powder puff impression. The coat should not be so long as to obliterate the natural outline. It would be impossible to really assess a dog's movement or proportions with a big, floppy mass of hair that was only lightly trimmed. On the other hand, a dog that is overtrimmed presents lines that are straight and harsh. Because they have not yet developed undercoat, puppies are often shown in short coat. This should be allowed for in the Puppy Classes, however, Bichons in any class other than Puppy should have sufficient coat texture to be shown in proper length and trim of coat.

Color: The standard is specific in stating the Bichon Frise is a white breed. Allowances are made, however, for shadings in small amounts. The very essence of the breed relies upon the black-white contrast the ideal specimen produces. Those specimens adherring to this picture should be encouraged.

Puppies are very often born with, or may develop color, especially about the head and ears. At times the color is surprisingly deep. By the time the individuals are a year or so old, most if not all of the color has disappeared.

It should be understood however that the allowance made for color is to be exercised with puppies only and not with adults. Any Bichon other than those shown in Puppy Class or those which are actually under 12 months should be penalized for excessive color.

Gait: The Bichon's movement in profile is above all effortless and ground covering. Furry little legs churning up a storm may appear to be going places but observing how much ground those legs cover is as important as how effortlessly they cover it. Coming and going there is only very slight convergence of the legs and then only when the dog is trotting at high speeds. The rearquarter movement of the Bichon is less wide than one might be accustomed to in other breeds. However, this does not mean to imply that he should move close behind. Close movement is defined as that in which there is distance between the upper legs but the leg, from hock to foot brushes against the other in movement.

Size: Equal consideration must be given to all Bichons where ever they might fall within the preferred size range, all other things being equal. It must be remembered that this could well include a top of the scale bitch or a bottom of the scale dog. The standard provides considerable latitude in order to include all superior specimens. Decisions should never be made on the basis of size alone as size constitutes only one small portion of the standard's requirements.

Temperament: Temperament is the barometer for assessing breed character. Shyness, agressiveness or sharpness are not characteristics of true Bichon temperament and should never be rewarded. The Bichon Frise is a companion dog, therefore his attitude should never be anything less than what is a joy to man.

Photo by Missy.

Ch. Crockerly Beau Monde Eclipse graces the cover of Kennel Review magazine in 1979. *Photo by Missy*

Chapter V
JUDGING THE BICHON FRISE

In order for this chapter to be of any value to those who read it, the reader must understand that I firmly believe a judge adjudicating in the ring has only one real duty and that is to find the best dogs in the ring and reward them on the basis of their merit. A breeder's job is no different. The breeder must be able to look at a litter or at potential breeding stock in the same manner. The question must always be, "How much good is there here?" and not, "What is wrong with this dog?"

If the answer to the first question is that there is little or no good in the dog being observed, there is no need to be concerned with faults. This allows the observer to then concentrate on the dogs of merit. Which of these has the most quality?

The question isn't, "which dog has cowhocks?" but rather, "which of these good dogs has the *best* rear quarters?" Looking for the faults in dogs is an exercise in futility. I can save the observer a great deal of time by quoting one of my greatest mentors, the late Beatrice Godsol, who said, "All dogs have faults, the great ones just carry them well."

So, how does the judge go about finding the best dogs? If the judge has a well written standard at hand and has prepared him or her self with a sound understanding of the basics of canine anatomy, the task is greatly simplified. But is that it? Is that all there is to becoming a top level judge? Unfortunately not so. These are only the first steps. If the key to top level judging were that simple than all judges would render a brilliant performance which, in case you may have noticed, is not always the case.

The very best judges have what the old timers always called "an eye for a dog." We went through what was fortunately a brief period in the 90s when certain individuals among the all breed powers that be, tried to discredit this belief. Their theory apparently was that proper ring procedure and a working knowledge of canine anatomy led one up the path to success as a judge. It didn't take long to prove their theory was more wishful thinking than reality. Ring procedure and a course in anatomy can enable an individual to recognize a good, sound, generic dog but breeding generic dogs is not what we as breeders are all about.

So, what about this "eye for a dog?"

This "eye" is really not quite as mystical or unique a gift as it might appear to be. It is quite simply an inherent appreciation for line, balance, and symmetry. All good artists have this gift as do many people whose only association with art is an appreciation of it.

AKC judge, Edd Bivin, commented further on this "gift," if one wishes to call it that. "The judge who has an eye," he said, "must also be able to articulate it." In other words, the judge must be able to express, by placing in proper order, that which he recognizes as quality.

There are things that can interfere with this articulation. Dr. Alvin Grossman, licensed Psychologist and prominent dog fancier and judge, wrote an award winning article (*"There's More Than Meets The Eye Inside The Squared Circle," Kennel Review Magazine*) in which he discusses some of the psychological factors that can impede the articulation of the "eye."

"As a Psychologist I have worked with people who, under stress, have not performed consistently or up to the best of their ability. In short they became erratic. At times such judges can be easily swayed while at other times they are adamant. A person who is basically indecisive in his reactions to life will also be an indecisive judge. He may know his breed but will have a terrible time making up his mind and thus can be swayed by factors extraneous to the dogs presented to him. Others may be forceful and dominant and brook no nonsense. They may also be unwilling to learn. There is the judge who is so poorly organized that he has no control of his ring and the resulting chaos allows for a poor presentation by the handler and dog.

"A judge whose personal problems interfere with his performance is to be avoided. However, judges do not wear ID tags that describe their state of mind. I believe we have such judges but there is literally no way to identify them at the time they are licensed. Also, these emotional problems may be transient and not seen again - the waking up on the wrong side of the bed syndrome.

"Then there is the judge whose own life has been unrewarding and who feels he has been shabbily treated by those in authority. This is the kind of person who relishes playing "God" in the ring. He enjoys knocking off the current big winner and being able to boast about it to the hometown folks later."

Then too there is the judge who becomes so overwhelmed by his study of canine anatomy that the parts of a dog take on greater significance than the whole. I have observed many a judge whose eye is immediately drawn to the best dog as the entry files in, but who soon loses sight of it as he begins to compare one dog's sickle hock against the other's bowed pastern. My advice to any judge who begins to see a dog as a series of interrupted parts is to shut his eyes, spin around three times, and start all over again. The parts only have value when they combine to make up the desired whole.

Even the judge who has an eye and is able to use it is not absolved from continuing his education; any more than having a sense of rhythm is all that is required for achieving success as a ballet dancer. Constant study and comparison, appreciation of the good ones that come before him and objectivity will constantly hone that "eye", making it all the more sensitive and reliable.

The 5 Components of Type

Learning to recognize generic canine soundness is the easy part. That is not said to minimize its importance. It is something all beginning students should master so that he or she can proceed on to begin their study of type. Only then can an individual fully recognize and appreciate what soundness means in a specific breed. We have a great number of dogs who move similarly but there is just as great a number to which general rules of soundness do not apply. It should be understood that the original purpose of some breeds did not include the efficient movement that is best recognized at a trot.

The efficient gate of the Sighthounds is the gallop. The Bulldog's purpose in life was never meant to be the same as the Greyhound's and therefore the Bulldog is built in a manner to perform in its own inimitable way. The way the breed is built determines how it shall move and if it does move in that way this and only this is what constitutes soundness for that breed.

Fortunately the Bichon Frise is a breed whose standard makes it quite clear as to what the breed should be and how it should perform. Just to make sure that it was not missed in previous chapters, I quote from the standard: "This is a breed that has no gross or incapacitating exaggerations and therefore there is no inherent reason for lack of balance or unsound movement."

It should be understood that the movement being referred to in the standard is that of a breed meant to move in a manner that is generally considered easy and efficient. This being the case, and with the student having completed his or her basic studies, we are then able to move on to type itself and what the word "type" actually means in dog parlance.

I am an ardent reader of the English newspaper *Dog World* and receive it by air mail every week. It is geared toward the breeder rather than toward the exhibitor as so many of the American publications are today. Hardly an issue goes by that I do not find some pearl of wisdom that requires making a special note of or clipping out for filing in my research library.

One article in particular by Sheila Atter, a regular columnist in that publication, struck a long lasting note with me. It is applicable to all breeds and particularly appropriate here, where we discuss judging of the Bichon.

In her article Atter makes the point that a person must fully understand what the elements are that are actually included in the word type if he or she is to recognize a typey dog when they see one. Otherwise the student wanders aimlessly through their life as a dog person, never really understanding what it is they are looking for or recognizing it when they do see it.

Her article started me thinking and led me to my own conclusions as to what is included in my definition of type in purebred dogs. After long and careful consideration I came up with a list of those characteristics with which I evaluate dogs and which the great dogs I have known have scored very heavily. They are:

1. Breed Character
2. Silhouette
3. Head
4. Movement
5. Coat.

We shall take a look at each in that order which would be my order of priority in this breed and are also very much the same order in which most judges are inclined to observe their dogs in the ring.

Breed Character: The most obvious thing about any dog when it enters the ring is whether or not it looks and acts as it should for that specific breed. Does it enter the ring with the attitude and deportment *that is correct for that breed?*

Frank Sabella, former successful handler, and now highly regarded judge, is often quoted as saying breed character is one of the most important things he looks for in evaluating a dog. Experienced fanciers have come to know exactly what he is referring to: the *sum total* of all those mental and physical characteristics that define not only what the breed should look like, but how it should act.

In our discussion of the Bichon head the point was made that the standard's measurements mean absolutely nothing if, in the end, the dog's expression does not say with exuberance, *"I am a Bichon!"* So it is with the whole dog. If we can not look at a dog and instantly recognize, by its general look and attitude, that it is a Bichon—then it *is not truly a Bichon*, in spite of what a pedigree and registration certificate might say. It lacks the essence of the breed, that which distinguishes it from all other breeds. The dog does not have breed character.

Silhouette: As I drive down the street what catches my eye and makes me look is the overall silhouette of a dog. What my eye tells my brain is that the animal I am looking at is a particular breed. Closer examination will undoubtedly reveal how good a specimen of the breed that particular dog is, but the closer the dog's silhouette comes to the ideal, the more quickly I will identify the breed and the more apt that dog is to be a quality individual. Therefore, it is the whole that classifies the breed and the details within that framework that tell me how closely the dog conforms to my interpretation of the ideal.

It is proportions that create the correct silhouette. Thus, all the years involved in study and research to determine the breed's correct proportions have not as one might say, been to naught! Proportions are something concrete. A neck which is one third the length of the body is something you can see. One third of the dog's body length is exactly that. One third *of anything* is exactly that. There is no mystery about it. And so it goes for the entire Bichon. Once you have taught yourself what the correct proportions are, you will be able to recognize the correct dogs by their silhouettes because the sum of all the correct parts made that silhouette!

It is important for a judge, for anyone, coming from smooth coated breeds, not to be deceived by the trim of the Bichon. Scissors can create any picture you want them to on a coated dog. What we are talking about here is *the body's* silhouette, not the silhouette of the hair dresser's art.

God gave us all hands and this is a good place to use them. A lot of hair on top of the Bichon's head is not what constitutes a long neck. The only thing that makes for a long neck is—you guess it—*a long neck!* In order for the silhouette to be accurate, the parts that created it must themselves be pretty close to being correct: the height to length balance must be there, muzzle to skull proportions must be in the right balance, the neck must be of the proper length and set. In most cases the dog that you observe as correct standing still, will also be pretty close to correct when moving about. If that silhouette is held in movement, the parts are not only there, they are also working correctly.

Head: Without its unmistakable face and that twinkling expression even the Bichon whose character and silhouette tells you it is a member of that breed would be a disappointment. There can be no argument with that. That head is part and parcel of what gives us our breed but understand, it is not all that distinguishes the breed.

Far too many people make the mistake of thinking a dog's head is all that what really determines type. It was all breed judge Derek Rayne who once said that a dog's breed should be recognizable if all we saw was its head looking over the fence at us. I wouldn't argue with that at all except that I would

Ch. Sea Star's Beau Brummel *Painting by Glazbrook*

have to add, "it is then the rest of the dog tells just how good an example of that breed it is."

Movement: The Bichon standard is quite precise in its description of the breed's movement. If a Bichon moves poorly it is usually due to the dog's construction. I am not talking about attitude, that is a matter of temperament I am talking about what the legs do or do not do. Whether or not the movement is ground covering and not just fast. Whether there is sufficient reach in the front and both drive and follow through behind.

A Bichon can only move properly if it is constructed properly. When you change construction you are tampering with breed type. It is not perfectly fine for one breed to move like another. A Bichon is not as fast as the Standard Poodle, nor should it be. Nor on the other hand is it as slow or does it waddle like the bull breeds. If all breeds were allowed to move in the same way, we would soon have a whole race of dogs differing only in size and color and the amount of hair they carry—quite simply "generic dogs."

There is too great an inclination to use the same yardstick to measure quality in vastly different breeds. One of those measurements is speed. For what ever the reason, exhibitors seem to think speed is an essential of a top winning show dog. It makes so little sense and yet one would think that if you can get a Bichon to move as fast as as an Irish Setter, you have a better Bichon. It is up to the judge to keep the dogs in his or her ring moving at a pace most suitable for the breed.

A dog forced to move beyond its proper speed will begin to exhibit faults which may or may not be there. It would be unfortunate for a judge to lose sight of the best dog in the ring simply because the judge did not insist that each dog be moved at the pace best suited to the breed and individual dog.

Sharon Newcomb, a long time breeder and judge of German Shepherds has been heard to say more than once to her exhibitors, "If you insist upon running that dog at full clip you can run it right out of my ring!" Wiser words have probably seldom been spoken.

Coat: In the case of the Bichon we are concerned with both color and texture. It would seem that white is white and it ends there. However, anyone who has tried to touch up a mar on a white wall will tell you that there are probably as many shades of white as there are colors in a rainbow. Bichon whites can range from a creamy white at one end of the scale to an ice white at the other end. The difference from dog to dog is usually quite subtle until the opposite ends of the spectrum are standing next to each other.

In so long as the Bichon being judged is in fact white and not cream, there is no need for concern. The standard is quite specific, however, in stating the color is *white* and even though it permits shadings of cream of buff, cream or apricot in specific areas around the ears and/or body, these shadings can only constitute 10% of the entire coat.

Most breeders are not concerned where, within the white spectrum, the individual Bichon might fall in that it appears even the far end extremes have value. Very often the coat of the ice white dog will be blessed with a beautiful tail plume and an ability to grow furnishings of exceptional length on the face and ears. In fact overall length of coat never seems to be a real problem with coats of this type. The down side seems to be in density. There is definitely an undercoat but both the inner and outer coats are comprised of hair that is a finer and silkier in nature.

The cream white coat on the other hand, has all the texture in the world but may present far more of a problem in developing the tail plume and facial hair necessary to complete the Bichon picture. The ideal coat of course is one that is midpoint between the two textures combining the desirable length and density.

In Summary

In order to be a good judge of the Bichon Frise whether it be in the ring or deciding upon breeding stock, one must use good sense and not let what knowledge they may have of the breed stand in the way of making wise choices. Because an individual can recognize a fault is no great accomplishment. Just where that fault is placed in context of the dog's overall makeup is what marks the knowledgeable judge or breeder.

In judging livestock of any kind the person making decisions must know the difference between what constitutes a real fault and what is simply a shortcoming. A judge who dismisses the best Bichon in the ring because its coat texture is not what it could be, is doing a disservice to the breed. The judge who overlooks characteristics of dwarfism in the Bichon because the dog has a pleasant expression or jaunty attitude, does serious harm to the breed.

The breeder can afford the luxury of dismissing a good dog because of some personal prejudice, he or she harms only their own breeding program. Those who officiate in the ring can not make their decisions based on personal whims. They do harm to the entire breed.

*Noted actress and animal lover, Betty White, is shown with guest Eve Arden and six Bichons, two of which are taking a nap, on the set of the popular television show, **Pet Set**, in 1969. The blonde lady in the background is Barbara Stubbs.*

Chapter VI
SUCCESS IN BREEDING BICHONS

TWENTY BASIC BREEDING PRINCIPLES
by Raymond Oppenheimer

The breeder is the backbone of the fancy and the importance of good breeding principals a top priority. England's master breeder, the late Raymond Oppenheimer is considered by the majority of dog fanciers to have been one of the world's most successful and knowledgeable breeders of purebred dogs. His "Ormandy" Kennels have a world-wide reputation for outstanding Bull Terriers. Although his "Twenty Basic Breeding Principles" were written originally for Bull Terriers, they are so sound and valuable they really encompass all breeds.

1. Don't make use of indiscriminate outcrosses. A judicious outcross can be of great value; an injudicious one can produce an aggregation of every imaginable fault of the breed.

2. Don't line breed just for the sake of line breeding. Line breeding with complimentary types can bring great rewards; with unsuitable ones it will lead to immediate disaster.

3. Don't take advice from people who have always been unsuccessful breeders. If their opinions were worth having they would have proved it by their successes.

4. Don't believe the popular cliche about the brother or sister of the great champion being just as good to breed from. For every one that is, hundreds are not. It depends on the animal concerned.

5. Don't credit your own dogs with virtues they don't possess. Self-deceit is a stepping stone to failure.

6. Don't breed from mediocrities. The absence of a fault does not in any way signify the presence of its corresponding virtue.

7. Don't try to line breed to two dogs at the same time; you will end by line breeding to neither.

8. Don't assess the worth of a stud bog by his inferior progeny. All stud dogs sire rubbish at times. What matters is how good their best efforts are.

9. Don't allow personal feelings to influence your choice of a stud dog. The right dog for your bitch is the right dog, whoever owns it.

10. Don't allow admiration of a stud dog to blind you to his faults. If you do. You will soon be the victim of auto intoxication.

11. Don't mate together animals which share the same fault. You are asking for trouble if you do.

12. Don't forget that it is the whole dog that counts. If you forget one virtue while searching for another, you will pay for it.

13. Don't search for the perfect dog as a mate for your bitch. The perfect dog (or even bitch) doesn't exist— never has, never will.

14. Don't be frightened of breeding from animals that have obvious faults, so long as they have compensating virtues. A lack of virtues is by far the greatest fault of all.

15. Don't mate together non-complementary types.

An ability to recognize type at a glance is a breeder's greatest gift. Ask the successful breeders to explain this subject - there's no other way of learning. (I'd define non-complementary types as ones which have the same faults and lack the same virtues.)

16. Don't forget the necessity to preserve head quality. It will vanish like a dream if you do.

17. Don't forget that substance plus quality should be one of your aims. Any fool can breed one without the other.

18. Don't forget that a great head plus soundness should be one of your aims. Many people can never breed either.

19. Don't ever try to decry a great Bull Terrier. A thing of beauty is not only a joy forever, but a great Bull Terrier should be a source of aesthetic pride and pleasure to all true lovers of the breed.

20. Don't be satisfied with anything but the best. The second best is never good enough.

Photo by Missy.

SELECTING THE FOUNDATION BITCH
by Karla Matlock

Phase I

Before selecting your brood stock, there is one major promise to make to yourself:

DON'T BE IN A HURRY!

Before doing anything in the way of selecting your foundation bitch, do your homework. Read and *understand* the standard for the breed. Call and visit local reputable breeders. Ask them questions and if you don't understand the answer, ask more questions. If the breeder is reputable he or she will show you their dogs and allow you to compare them against the standard. But most importantly, they will discuss with you the various types within the breed and discuss with you why those types fit or do not fit the standard.

Ask about health problems the breeder has seen. Do they check hips, eyes, knees? Do they have documentation to back up their health claims?

Visit as many breeders as possible and do not be in a hurry. Go out to look and learn, with the actual purchase of a bitch being way down the current list of priorities. Education in the breed, the standard and the genetic pool should top this list.

Go to dog shows and meet people and look at dogs. Compare them in your minds eye to the standard you have now read and understand. Attend Bichon specialty shows and visit with breeders/owners. Listen to them and ask more questions. But keep in mind, ALL dog owners have their own opinions, likes, dislikes, and preferences. All this accumulated information must now be assimilated and deciphered.

After accomplishing all of these things, you should now have a list of the qualities you are in search of:

Head — short muzzle, long muzzle, medium muzzle?

Eye — big, round, almond, black, brown?

Front — straight, toe-out, slightly out?

Temperament — 'laid back', outgoing, tough, mellow?

With your education, you should be able to answer these questions and know what your program needs and what it does not need. These are questions only you can answer with the good of your program at heart. But, remember, we are all still looking for the perfect Bichon!

In researching your brood selection, pedigree can play an important role. Go back at least four generations and look at the stock behind the bitch. Find people that knew, saw and used that stock. Find their breeders and do not be afraid to ask the questions only the breeder can answer. Have the get been quality animals and successful in their endeavors (i.e. in the ring or as producers)? Are the quality percentages low? Why?

Are the get all spayed and neutered pets? Were they shown to their championship? Why did the dogs turn out the way they did? The answers to these questions will lead you to decisions important to your future in your program. The answers will also lead you to another important discovery: a mentor.

Phase II

Your mentor should be knowledgeable, understanding and honest enough to answer those "tough to admit" questions. Someone you can trust not only with your breeding program, but with the future and well-being of the breed. Someone that knows what lines blend and what line, once blended, can lead to disaster. This should be someone who knows the breed, has used outside lines, and can readily recognize the success and/or failure of blended lines. Talking to great breeders of any breed will assist you in selecting your foundation bitch.

Your foundation bitch is not necessarily a great show dog. Actually, she may be ordinary or average in many ways and not always great in others. If she comes from good stock and a reputable breeder, you can feel safe that, bred properly, the qualities she has, combined with the selection of a compatible gene pool, will yield quality and will preserve the longevity of the breed.

Now the research of the breed, your understanding of the standard, and the advice of your mentor is complete. The checklist is finished and the hunt and/or wait for "Madam X" begins. Most reputable breeders keep their puppies a minimum of 12 weeks before grading the litter. The show dogs and the pet puppies are selected by the breeder. At this point, do not let anxiety overwhelm you. In some cases, your show quality puppy may be four-to-six months old before the breeder lets her go. During this time, the puppy can change on a daily basis. Good breeders are watching bites, pigment, and general confrmation carefully.

Phase III

Your "young lady" is selected and delivered. She is s turning out to be a nice little dog. The handling classes and puppy classes are going well. This is the first phase of enjoying the aspect of being an owner/handler. First the enjoyment and feelings of self-satisfaction can not be measured as your little lady progresses. The hard work, the laughter and the tears make it all worthwhile.

During this time, you should also continue your education. Continue to visit breeders, visit dog shows and learn from the things you see and hear. Continue to compare dogs against the standard. Continue to communicate with your mentor.

Visiting dog shows during this time as an owner-handler is a valuable aspect to your program. These are the dogs you may want to use as studs in the future. When you have the opportunity to see them for yourself, you do not have to rely on the word of any one else as to the visual qualities of the dog. *Do not leave your breeding program in the hands of anyone else.*

If handling your bitch in the showring is not your cup ot tea using a professional handler is a good idea. However, this should not keep you from attending the shows to see what else is out there. There is not only one great breeder, one great dog or one great bloodline. Knowledge of other lines is your responsibility as a good breeder.

By this time, you should know your bitches' weaknesses and strengths. You should be aware of the qualities you want to bring into your program. You should be ready to begin the search for "Mr. Romeo" and should be able to recognize the qualities he possesses

Ch. Beau Monde Drewlaine Durango surrounded by some wannabees.

to enhance your program. As you do all this, continue to ask questions while continuing your search for the "perfect mate". Begin the weeding out process of dogs that are not compatible with the traits you hope to bring into your program. Do not let distance be a factor in not seeing a particular dog. You must see him for yourself. Don't rely on rumor, innuendo and hearsay. Go and see for yourself. Try, if at all possible, to watch the ring for his previous offspring. Find out what bitches he has been bred to and compare them with yours. If they are comparable to your girl, what were the strengths and weaknesses of the puppies from those breedings? Are they something you may see in your program? Are they something you do not want to see in your program?

As your bitch continues to mature, monitor her strengths and weaknesses continually. Look for dogs that are strong where your bitch is weak. Decide if the stud's strong characteristics are going to add to your program without sacrificing the strong characteristics you already have. Try to lock in strong points, such as pigment, before worrying about adding something minor. Normally, line-breeding will lock these traits, whereas an outcross may bring you a surprise. The outcross breeding may result in traits that are difficult to trace and could have come from either side of the pedigree.

Remember that the top-producing dams are usually average bitches. In talking with many breeders, I have found that often the 'ugly duckling' produces wonderful get. Behind an 'ugly duckling' there could be a beautiful swan. But this premise is based upon the gene pool available to both the dog and the bitch.

I believe that a great foundation bitch can be bred in a number of ways and always produce a better litter. A bitch bred to the same male four times, producing great puppies each time only means that the gene pools 'connected'. But where do you go from there? No one wins.

However take the same bitch and, based upon your acquired knowledge and preparation, breed her to four different males. If the results are great puppies, your program is now laid out for generations ahead. These puppies can remain in your program and offer various qualities they have acquired from the combined gene pools.

Phase IV

Once your girl's Championship is finished, she should have her eyes tested by a certified ophthomologist and her hips cleared by the Orthopedic Foundation for Animals (OFA). Her knees (stifles) should be cleared and a Bucellocis test given. Isolate a number of prospective stud dogs and request pedigrees. Get the results of the same tests you put your girl though, select the 'lucky guy', sign your contract and it's time to breed.

After sixty-three (plus or minus) days, your puppies are here. Cute little bundles of hair, but the vigil just now starts. For the first four-to-five weeks, let them be puppies. Let them grow, play and start to mature. Many changes occur in this time, so don't be alarmed.

At four-to-six weeks, start the bathing and trimming of eyes and feet. Get them used to one of their lots in life. At eight weeks, full grooming should begin, developing the distinguished look of becoming a *Bichon*.

Now you can see the balance starting to form: leg, neck, chest, coat, movement. This is where a true puppy area is needed. An area giving them enough room to romp and run, yet accessible enough to allow you to administer the handling, cuddling and general TLC they all need.

By about twelve weeks, some pets in the litter may become obvious and are placed with wonderful, loving people. But this is the same age when you begin to watch for the "great white hope." That perfect, or as near to perfect as possible, Bichon.

Always plan ahead for your program. If the 'right' puppy owner does not come along, do not panic. As breeders will tell you, Murphy's Law will strike you sooner or later. No one knows what lies around the corner and all things happen for a reason. You know the puppies are quality and, as we discussed before, based on your knowledge and research, this puppy should fit right back into your program. After all, why are you breeding if not to continue with another good one.

If you were led astray and the litter is a disaster, cut your losses. It may be quite difficult to start over, but start over you must. Fine tune your program. It may be something as simple as the wrong stud for this particular bitch or some other discernible flaw. Consult other breeders and your mentor. Find out why and work to fix the problem. The more you learn, the wiser you become. Remember, as a responsible reputable breeder, you are here to preserve and improve the integrity of the breed.

Keep in mind that every line has its problems. Unfortunately, bad genetics are behind all of our programs. FACT: It depends on how we combine the genes that will make the difference. If the bitch is bred twice, to different lines, and both litters produce nothing better than the dam or sire, spaying may be the only option. In that case, return to Phase I and begin again.

Your goal should not be to breed for pet quality animals. You nust breed for the best, *each and every time*. Take every measure to try and guarantee it. But remember, you can not fool Mother Nature. Do not set your sights too high or expect unreasonable results.

As a final thought, I asked myself what I would do if I were to start over in this breed. I decided that I would never let distance stand in my way. After learning the standard and knowing the standard, I would see as many dogs as possible. I would not be so trusting and I would study harder to learn more about the breed.

I would buy, even the first time, from an individual that would be my mentor and not expect me to be theirs. I would see every animal I could from the line I was considering. I would compare the qualities and faults. I would look for consistency.

Remember, you can never know all there is to know about this breed. Gene pools may be limited, but learn all you can. As a responsible, reputable breeder, you must breed for the best, *each and every time*.

Photo by Lawrence.

THE STUD DOG
by Pauline Schultz

It is interesting how differently our thought processes and programs can be from someone elses and yet our ultimate goals and accomplishments can be strikingly similar. So it is with human beings and with Mother Nature herself.

In the perfect world all Bichons would be the same type and size with a totally correct head and coat and completely sound in every respect. Unfortunately we do not live in a perfect world and we have no access to perfect dogs. Therefore, we try to create that illusive "great one."

My own personal breeding program has been based on breeding extreme to extreme. If my bitch is extreme I look for the stud dog with the opposite extreme. This has always given me better substance and balance.

If you are looking for a particular quality in an outcross stud dog (let us say the correct large eye) you must, of course, use the dog that has the eye you after. But he alone is not the deciding factor. His pedigree must be made up of individuals that have that same quality. He must be heavily linebred in order to pass on this quality you are seeking.

Do not forget however, that you may well get the rest of what his gene pool carries: whether it be coat, angulation, overall type or what-have-you. His pedigree might just as easily be lacking in any or all of these respects. Therefore it is very important that he and his pedigree will give you more than just the proper eye. Do not sacrifice everything else for improvement in just a single area.

If your bitch is the result of a loose or outcross breeding, the stud you select for her should be heavily line bred with a preponderance of the qualities you seek and he will undoubtedly dominate the resulting puppies.

If your bitch is heavily line bred to the style you prefer and you are using a male from a different line you may want to choose a stud that is not as tightly bred. This will assist you in not straying too far from where you are.

Experience has taught me that it is relatively easy to change certain characteristics in your breeding program yet others can be extremely resistant to change. Heads, eyes, tail sets, angulation, balance or coat can at times be changed in a single breeding. On the other hand correct fronts, once lost, may take generations to straighten out if they are ever corrected at all.

What a "head breed" we have! The Bichon's beautiful face and expression can melt your heart and I love them. However, a Bichon does not walk on its head and a lovely head on a poorly balanced, unsound body is such a waste.

The correct profile movement of our breed is so beautiful and is as distinctive as it is efficient. You must look for that in your stud dog even though you are breeding for that beautiful head. The reach and drive is so effortless it appears as though the little dog could do this all day long without tiring. It can only come from balanced angulation front and rear.

If the dog you are considering breeding to is one that produces well laid back shoulders and correct length of upper arm he is worth his weight in gold. His contribution to your breeding program can be immeasurable.

Many dogs can produce pretty but few are able to pass on correct structure.

Ch. Beau Monde Miss Chaminade, owned by Richard G. Beauchamp and Barbara Stubbs. Photo by Missy.

SELECTING A SHOW PUPPY
by Barbara Stubbs

I wish I were one of those who say they are able to look at a puppy at the moment of birth and say "Aha! Without question this will be a show dog." My, how convenient this would be. I am not that fortunate. Of course I cannot resist the temptation to mentally evaluate a litter during those early weeks when the eyes open, they discover they have legs and individual personalities begin to emerge.

A six week old puppy gives me a hint at what is to come (and they are certainly never more appealing!) but at eight weeks there is a reality check and I become serious about considering the width of skull, length of muzzle, eye placement and of course pigmentation and coat type. Length of neck, body proportion and tail sets are visually evident at this juncture as well. If you can convince an energetic eight week old Bichon he should stand for thirty-seven seconds you can confirm with your hands the shoulder layback and rear angulation, or lack thereof, you have witnessed as he has moved about.

Watching the youngsters move is fundamental. If you can be on their level without their knowing they are being watched you have an ideal situation. Their interaction and the resulting movements can be extremely revealing. Here you will determine whether there are exaggerations, either positive or negative, and if that overall balance you are seeking is actually there.

Ten weeks brings another evaluation primarily to see if your assessments of the individuals made at eight weeks are still valid. To me twelve weeks is the end of Phase One. Occasionally there are disappointments and often some question marks. Has that muzzle really gotten longer? Was the loin quite that long? Usually the puppy that showed enormous promise at both eight and ten weeks will continue to hold your interest at twelve weeks. However, the fellows that were of interest at eight weeks but less at ten weeks may continue that trend.

There is an additional factor that is at the top of many lists when considering a show puppy, that of TEMPERAMENT. Puppies in a given litter have varying temperaments regardless of environmental uniformity. But only those with that special outgoing perspective will be ultimately successful as a showdog. From day one every breeder looks for the unique puppy that exudes that indefinable quality that not only catches the eye, but holds it! Therein lies the essence of it all.

To regress a moment. "Selecting a Show Puppy." This suggests we are selecting a puppy which at greater maturity will compete in the show ring successfully and eventually achieve its' championship. Herein lies the problem.

People new to the show world invariably want a puppy no older than three months with a virtual guarantee this youngster will hypnotize the world on his ultimate debut. Obviously this is unrealistic considering the number of variables involved, not least of which is the novice owner himself! When considering puppies at this age the most one can honestly offer is a "Show Prospect."

It has been my experience that four to six months is the most frustrating developmental interval of all. Temperaments are generally consistent but everything else seems to go awry. Every part of those little bodies seems to be operating under a different growth pattern; the stylish little fellow of twelve weeks can become hardly recognizable during this period. An interlude of panic may ensue.

Then as the six to seven month period arrives the proportions begin to come together once again, albeit more slowly in some than others. The puppy that caught your attention months before, does so again. You will be closer to confirming those areas that seriously establish show potential; muzzle and head proportions, width of skull, strength of expression, length of neck, shoulder layback and rear angulation, correct leg proportion and length of loin with the strong tail set that completes the picture. Once again "balance" is a key word.

From eight or nine months to twelve months and the end of "official" puppyhood, the maturation process is generally less dramatic than the earlier stages. Coat improvement is especially noticeable as the developing undercoat increases the density and the scissored pattern actually holds! In general this is a delightful time to enjoy the growing youngster; scattered moments of adulthood followed by quick regression to "basic puppy." A challenge for all.

Whether a "Show Prospect" is selected at three months or at six months of if one opts for the greater security of choice that comes when selecting a "teenager," several environmental factors influence their development; generally happy surroundings, of course, plus exercise and conditioning, nutrition, happy training, socialization and more socialization. Sounds obvious? I am astounded at how often it is NOT. A talented handler will see that his dog performs adequately and points will be won. But the difference between a show dog and a SHOW DOG can be the cumulative effects supplied by a positive environment during those all-important puppy days.

The "Specials Dog"? How do you define that? "Special" is an apt label, for those that are truly successful have, in addition to quality, an aura that gives you pleasure when you see them. Their enthusiasm is contagious. There is an acknowledged bond between dog and handler. But there is something extra in the heart of those "special" dogs that makes them love the spectacle and communicates that fact to those who watch. Occasionally...oh, very occasionally...one of those Show Puppies grows up and crosses that line from "very nice show dog" to enter the realm of those with that extraordinary focus and marvelous appeal. It is indeed, "Special."

Photo by Missy.

OWNER-HANDLING YOUR DOG
Versus
USING A PROFESSIONAL
by Mary and Kathie Vogel

Vogelflight first started breeding and exhibiting Miniature Schnauzers in the late 1960s. We felt that owner-handling our particular breed at that time was far from satisfying due to several factors. Majors within a four hour drive were impossible to find plus the 'timing' of the Schnauzer's coat was difficult. A calender is needed to determine what date your dog's coat will be "in" coat and ready to show. Consequently there was little choice of which shows you could enter and the judges you would have.

In the later sixties and seventies, the mid-west Chicago area was the hub for the Schnauzer and major points were not a problem. Consequently, we found ourselves sending our dogs to the professionals in that area but having shown and bred our own horses prior to entering the world of dogs, we found this arrangement less than satisfying.

The lack of 'on the scene' participation left us with too many questions: How well did our dog show? Was he presented correctly? Did he deserve to win or to lose? What was the quality of his competition? Which judges' opinion should we respect? Obviously the questions could not be answered because *we were not there.*

The above are all the reasons we made the decision to consider a different breed of dog. We wanted one that we could personally show without the 'coat timing' problems that we mentioned and also a breed that would not also seasonally drop its coat.

In our search, we considered several interesting breeds but finally the Bichon Frise won our admiration and dedication. It was charming, intelligent, hardy and once in coat and pattern, could be shown at our own discretion. The added attraction was that this was a new breed to this country and we could be a part of its development.

At the time we acquired our first Bichons there was not a unified grooming pattern that the fanciers agreed upon. In fact, many said absolutely *no* scissoring! Within a very short time we started exhibiting in rare breed shows hoping to meet fellow breeders and exhibitors and to share our views. In the beginning, most of the Bichons entered looked like fluffy blimps. We appreciated balance and movement too much to be satisfied with just scissor tipping the coat.

Having groomed the Schnauzer, we started scissoring the legs in the same cylinder pattern and taking the hair tighter on the rear legs just to the point of hock and following the contour of the dogs body conformation. Viola! We had a pattern. Of course, over the years the pattern has become tighter and the head trim has gone from an elongated bell to a shorter version. However, the totally round "Westie look" is incorrect. The Bichon has a drop ear, not a prick ear. Why try to make it appear otherwise? This is very important for the true Bichon expression.

Within the same time frame, on the West Coast, Barbara Stubbs, Richard Beauchamp and Frank Sabella were trimming in the same manner. This was not a coincidence but a happening because it was the logical pattern to use, following the dog's structure.

Now to the shows! To be a successful owner-handler, you must have confidence and present and handle your dog correctly. That much is obvious but also, your dog must be good, make that *better*, than the handlers! While the professional may have the upper hand by having more experience, you the breeder and owner should have the better eye for the dog. After all, you created your dog, now sell it to the judges! Quite often, some breeders turn their lesser quality dogs over to a professional. Too bad, but this practice is not uncommon.

The main ingredient to being a successful owner-handler is quality, quality, quality! Whenever seen in the ring, you must be seen with the best. Set your standards high, stop counting the number of champions you have bred or owned, instead, consider how outstanding your finished dogs are. If parent clubs would stop awarding club members for numbers, perhaps we would have fewer inferior champions.

Most novice owners are at a disadvantage going up against the "Pros" where a coated breed is concerned. The professional is usually more talented with the scissors. With the trim, you can help disguise a fault or you can make a good dog look as if he has serious faults. We think the latter is the weakness of many owner-handlers. This is not to say that our breed does not have its share of owners that possess the "scissors gift." One only has to attend our National Specialty to be aware of the gifted.

Dog shows are just that - shows. Showmanship is important in any breed and we do not feel we are breed prejudiced by stating that the Bichon ring is one of the most popular rings watched at all breed shows. And why not! They are very entertaining. Expect the unexpected! They are beautiful to the eye and when properly structured, they have a uniquely flowing movement.

The owner-handler should remember that the professional seldom has the luxury of having superior class dogs. Unless their dog is a "Specials Dog" the handler does not have time to pick and choose judges or show site for a particular class dog. The class dog becomes one of many and the majority rules.

Owner-handlers can avoid a particular judge they feel is either political or just doesn't have a true understanding of our breed. It is imperative that breeders not support poor judges, the only exception being if it is a specialty show. Specialties are for the breeders to show their puppy hopefuls to fellow breeders. It is a time to present their breeding program and to view others. The Specialty is also the breeders' opportunity to examine the stud dogs that they have been considering and to exchange views, pedigrees and to discuss specific breed problems.

Mind you, we are not trying to criticize the professionals because they are needed by many owners and the successful ones excel in their profession. They more than earn their fees. Still, they often lack that very special rapport that should exist between a dog and its owner, and this is understandable with class dogs.

A professional and his Specials Dog is another story. How many owners would, or could, travel and personally handle their dogs two to four days of every week for sometimes two years!? How many have the know-how for Group and Best in Show competition?

In summary, the owner-handler should perfect his grooming and handling skills. Set yourself a goal to become recognized as an owner of consistently quality dogs.

In time, the judges and professionals will respect your dedication and you will be able to stand competively (and proudly) behind your own dog.

Photo by Missy.

CAMPAIGNING THE SPECIALS DOG
by Lois Morrow

Once upon a time...that's a good way to begin an article on campaigning a Bichon Frise Special. Most of the "once upon a time" tales have heroes, heroines, villains, monsters, laughter and tears, stardust and sawdust. So goes "Specialing" if you're really serious about it. If you're content with just seeing your dog in competition, win or lose, congratulations, you've jumped straight to the Prince slipping the glass slipper on Cinderella's foot and don't have to be concerned with the mean stepmother, stepsisters and the midnight deadline. The real fairy tale comes with watching the standout puppy in the litter develop week by week, to become a beautiful, self assured adult who goes into the show ring and says, "I'm here to win" and does. There may still be a few villains, tears or sawdust along the way, but all fairy tales have to have those, too.

What does it take to make a Bichon a Special and not just a champion? If I had to answer that in one word, I would say "attitude." Temperament could be substituted for attitude. But, and that is a LARGE BUT, only if that dog is as close to the standard from nose to tail, standing still or moving, as we can breed. We have all finished dogs that are "good" but because of a less than correct front or rear, light eye or whatever, are just that, only good. That dog, or bitch, might have a place in a breeding program if the problem is slight and can be bred out, but it should not be shown as a Special. This is where the novice needs to get advice from knowledgeable breeders and handlers who will give them a truthful critique. Facing up to the facts early on can save wear and tear on your heart and bank account. Just consider how many Bichons become champions every year. How many of those can win Best of Breed consistently?

Many years ago, before I got into Bichons, someone remarked to me at Westminster that there are people who have shown dogs there for 50 years and never won the breed. At that time I thought, "Wow, it must really be hard to win there". Now, my thoughts would run more to, "they must not be breeding properly or showing the dogs well to not win even one Best of Breed in 50 years!"

On to that word "attitude". Take a beautifully presented dog, every hair in place, wonderful head, striucture and sound movement - a great picture. But, does he go in the ring and say, "Here I am, and I'm the best"? Or does he just come in the ring, stand nicely and go around the ring at whatever pace is asked of him, but would be just as happy in his crate or ex-pen?

I've tried a few out who have done the latter, and it's heartbreaking. Just hope they can produce something equally sound and good and work on developing the potential for attitude early on. This might be the place to answer the often asked question of which I would rather special, a dog or a bitch. I'd have to say a dog.

The male temperament generally seems to hold up better under the stress. The occasional bitch who has an extra bit of the male hormone testosterone seems to hold up well. However, a male is likely thinking he may find a bitch in season at the show. The bitch is thinking of the corner of the couch at home. Too often in Bichons, a good bitch is passed over for Best of Breed.

If a handler is needed, what would I look for? Someone who genuinely likes and respects dogs. Someone who is respected in the dog community. Go to dog shows and watch the Bichon ring. Which handler consistently has clean, well groomed dogs? Do the dogs and the handler appear to be happy and work well together? Does the handler appear competitive? He gets paid, win or lose.

Group and Best in Show wins come with an extra charge, but only a fool would complain about paying for them. Check out the handlers' setups. Does the handler have able assistants? Is each dog given a pat or a kind word along the way? Bichons really need a lot of this. Talk to other exhibitors who have used handlers.

This is a live dog, not an inanimate object. Choose carefully. Generally the dog will be going off to stay with the handler. Check out the facilities. The handler may have a dog of another breed in the Non Sporting group. That dog may have precedence over your dog and yours may go into the Group with an assistant on the lead if the other dog wins its breed. Is this OK with you?

Get a rate card from the handler so you know just what the charges will be. You will be paying a percentage of the travel expenses as well.

Somewhere along the line the handler will want to see your dog. Watch your dog's reaction. This first meeting is NOT final decision time.

Our "JP" upon first seeing Bill McFadden put his tail down and planted all four feet on the ground. Bill spoke kindly to him, picked him up, carried him to a table and fed him chicken breast. He didn't try to force him in any way and thus began the JP loves Bill, Bill loves JP saga.

It's interesting to note that Bill had never trimmed or handled a Bichon before JP. He had had a lot of success with a Kerry Blue and I felt if he could trim that breed he could do a Bichon. It is extremely important that your handler be able to trim your dog to your satisfaction. You know what you are breeding to produce and you want those qualities to show. Just a few hairs on or off in the wrong places can appear to destroy everything you've worked to produce. The pattern must suit the dog.

The handler's greatest responsibility is to the welfare of the dog - mental and physical. One of my Specials once spent 45 minutes being scissored to a beautiful smoothness. I appeared at the setup then and was told to keep him standing so every hair would stay in place. It was a large show and the handler had a lot of dogs, each of which was to be delivered to him at ringside by the assistant. It was 2 hours and 15 minutes until Bichons went in the ring! When no one was looking I took the dog out of the noose and he laid down and slept for 2 hours!

Fifteen minutes before ring time I gave him a drink, dried his beard, combed out the hocks and off to ringside he went. He went in - and won! (Not too many hairs were out of place.) The whole point of this little scenario is that you want to be sure the handler who takes your dog is going to have sufficient help to accommodate the number of dogs he or she shows. Dog shows should not have to be an endurance contest for your Special!

Every handler has good days and bad, but it makes sense to get to as many shows as possible to see what is going on. There is no way that any handler can guess what is important to you. You must communicate your wishes!

If your Special is winning and you want it to continue it is important to advertise. There are a lot of publications and it can be quite expensive to use more than a few. Use only good photos. Better no photo than a bad one.

Photos, photos, boy, do I have photos! Good ones, bad ones, taken on sunny days, windy days, even rainy days. The rainy day Bests in Show are works of art, thanks to the handlers. I especially like candid photos and often use those in advertising. Going through old pictures is a walk down memory lane. Lots of good times.

And the trophies. Winged victory trophies (dog on top of pedestal, the bigger the win the higher the pedestal) seem to be a thing of the past, thankfully. I so still have the first Group win trophy, a winged victory won by Ch. Chaminade Tempo, lo these many years ago. I haven't kept every trophy, but I do have a good many, and they are used. Much of the silver and crystal is displayed in a wonderful floor to ceiling cabinet. Black background, glass shelves, and lighting on a rheostat - a great look for a nighttime party.

My husband tells guests they're his golf trophies, then admits the dogs won almost all of them. Even "non doggy" people are impressed.

The retired challenge trophy bowls are on a cabinet in the great room, the center one filled with a large silk flower arrangement. Yes, the bases, with the dogs' names, are under them. Each room in the house has some "trophy", perhaps just a small silver box or ceramic. Armatel, that wonderful non-polish wonder, goes to our ranch in Idaho, along with the Pendleton blankets (I love them) and the more "rustic" things. I've been asked who decorated our houses - the dogs! (Thank you, you innovative trophy chairmen.) I'm surrounded by all these glorious memories.

The dogs, from Tempo through JP, have all come home to live out their lives as part of the family. My heart can still miss a beat when one of them, especially at 10 plus years, strides from one end of the dog yard to the other, flowing freely, head up, tail clamped on the back - just going from here to there.

The special friends, still fast through so many years, are like family. There are so many great people in dogs, some ever so knowledgeable, and so many just great fun to be with. Pick and choose carefully. Those who want to "arrange" things are the ones to back off from. I love to win, but I want wins that are deserved. Those you can savor. And with the right dog, they will come to you.

Ch. Sea Star's Another Valentino (far left) charms the passerbys, photographed by Holloway. On the left, patiently awaiting their turn and above, photo by Missy.

Chapter VII

THE BREEDERS SPEAK

The following five questions were posed to Bichon breeders:

1. Which Bichon Frise, not owned or bred by you, do you consider the closest to the Standard? Why?

2. Which Bichon owned and/or bred by you was most instrumental in helping you to achieve your goals? Why?

3. In the quest for coat and glamor in the modern Bichon, have conformation and movement been affected in any way?

4. What characteristics in particular do you consider essential to Bichon type?

5. What do you consider the greatest challenge that faces the breed at the present time? How do you feel it should be dealt with?

Their responses follow.

Miriam Barnhardt
Miri-Cal Bichons

I thought **Ch. Vogelflight's Music Man** (of course, a son of Mr. Beau Monde) was especially nice. I didn't breed to him as he was not available at the time as he was in Hawaii, so I bred to his brother, Choir Master, of the same gene pool. The get were more solid than my earlier breedings. Choir Master wasn't as outgoing as Music Man, but a nice dog.

I am admittedly a face, head and front freak and still find it's the first thing I look at, although I should have learned by now with such a great patella problem in the breed that rears are very important, I just made sure mine were x-rayed and knees checked before breeding and then went on from there, looking at heads, faces and fronts.

Yes, I think the quest for coat and glamour has greatly affected the breed. The coats have been used to cover up so many defects and judges have not helped by being afraid to put their hands on the dogs for fear of mussing the coat and incurring the handler's wrath.

One of our greatest challenges right now is size. We will end up as the Poodles have, fine boned and long legged with a division in size. I believe the nine and a half to eleven and a half in proportion is a good standard. I wouldn't be bothered one bit by a judge calling for a wicket.

At one time I raised different breeds of hunting dogs: English Setters, Beagles and then German Shepherds (look what happened to them!). Bichons are far removed from these, people tend to forget what some dogs are bred for. If a Bichon isn't flying around the ring then it's not considered a good, sound dog.

Mine do just fine jumping on chairs, sofas, peoples' laps and they run in the yard a mile a minute - *without* elongated legs.

Rosemarie Blood
Crockerly Bichons

In the early years, the greatest impact on the breed was created with the union of **Ch. Chaminade Mr. Beau Monde** and **Ch. C & D Countess Becky**. Type was set and the influence of Ch. Reenroy's Amy du Kilkany on facial expression, is still felt today.

Some of the dogs and bitches who came close to the Standard in the early days were:

Ch. Vogelflight's Music Man; Ch. Beau Monde The Huckster who gave us some style and elegance; Ch. Teeny Teepee's Chief of Diamdee who passed on soundness and stable temperaments.

In more recent years, among others were the very exciting and popular:

Ch. Devon's Puff 'N Stuff, Ch. Chaminade Larkshire Lafitte, Ch. Dovecoat's Mr. Magoo and Am.Can.Ch. Donsi's Snowbird, the latter an incredibly correct bitch that with limited showing, achieved some excellent wins.

My foundation was established with Ch. C & D Beau Monde Moonshine ROM, a healthy, stable and very typey bitch who produced two litters totaling fifteen puppies with nine of them Champions. Three were in the Top Ten for about three years. The delightful Miss Crystal (Ch. Crockerly's Beau Monde Eclipse) was one of those offspring.

Some of the lines that helped the breed along with their impact are: Beau Monde, Chaminade-Chamour, C & D, Paw Mark and Dovecoat.

Coats today are quite good everywhere in the show ring. Coat care and nutrition have more to do with a beautiful coat than anything else. Since I have had Bichons (twenty-five years), there have been varying coat textures but never a bad coat.

Soundness of body and mind, intelligence and a happy, joyful attitude with the ability to perform, these are the Hallmarks of the breed. If they are missing, there is nothing left to evaluate, regardless how good the body looks. If there is a good temperament, the correct Bichon expression, black pigment, correctly set, round, large, dark eyes would put the icing on the cake.

After twenty-five years of exhausting the limited gene pool, it is most important to reestablish long, healthy lines, along with the brainpower this breed is capable of exhibiting.

We need to make use of genetic guidance to eliminate afflictions and illnesses, establishing genetic pedigrees and educating breeders in their breeding practices.

Be true to the breed and yourself, the rest will take care of itself.

Mayree Butler
Reenroy Bichons

Ch. Vogelflights Music Man would have to be the one to come closest to the standard. Not only did Banjo qualify in every area of conformation, but he also maintained that excellent quality - not one of those early bloomers who failed to retain their appearance in later years. Also he was able to transmit these qualities to his get.

Reenroy's Riot Act was the most instrumental in my breeding program. Once again, his outstanding qualities were visible for generations.

Now we come to the real meat of this piece. It would seem that most of today's major breeders have forgotten the very basic premise that when one facet is altered, another is also subject to change without control.

In striving for "more leg" they have been willing to forego chest and strong fronts.

Their efforts to shorten the muzzle have resulted in undershot, overshot and level bites. You might remember from the 1995 National the comment that the level bite was "not as serious" as light eyes. In my book they are equal faults.

The fact that size is being totally ignored is of special concern to me. The Standard opens with the phrase "small, sturdy dog", and yet breeders are knowingly propagating thirteen inch and fourteen inch, twenty-five pound monsters which unknowledgeable judges put up for major wins.

Essential to Bichon type? - personality, personality, personality.

Most of this last question I covered above, but something must be done about the quality of the current judges. With AKC's relaxed requirements, too many simply don't know the basic conformation points and instead rely on the professional handlers. Educating the judges is essential.

Gertrude Fournier
Cali-Col Bichons

You asked which Bichons not owned by me do I consider closest to the standard and why. Since you did not specify past or present I presume you mean "presently." It immediately comes into my mind not one, but two lovely bitches, both bred by Mary and Kathy Vogel - **Ch. Vogelflight's Baudier Tulip** and **Ch. Vogelflight's Banana Pudding**. From ringside they are very similar but the judge can find differences. Tulip is a little smaller and moves differently from Pudding, who is typier and cobbier, but both have beautiful round heads, so notable in Vogelflight bitches, with round, dark eyes set wide apart; surrounded by dark pigment, gorgeous, ample white coat, and a joyful, merry temperament, so reminiscent of the Cali-Col Bichons. They represent the Bichon Standard as it should be. No short back and long legs! Balanced!

As for my own Bichons, I was fortunate to have bred many fine Champion males and bitches. But foremost, I must cite my **Sha-Bob's Nice Girl Missy**, who was not my breeding. Today she is listed as one of the all time, top producing dams with ten Champions to her credit. She was a sound bitch with flawless temperament and movement, and a dense, white coat. By today's Standard she was too long in body. She had beautiful carriage, and with her lovely tail carried over her back, she was a picture as she floated around the ring. Her puppies became foundation stock in the hands of careful breeders who even today can trace their line to her.

I cannot leave this without mentioning **Mex. Can. Ch. Cali-Col's Shadrack**, acclaimed by the late, well known Curtis Brown (who wrote several books on canine movement). He stated that Shadrack epitomized perfect Bichon movement. Unfortunately, Shadrack was not appreciated by many in the fancy, but in his short life he proved his outstanding ability to be a prepotent stud in siring consistent quality and type regardless of the different bitches bred to him.

Certainly conformation and movement have been

affected in the quest for coat and glamour. Since "bigger is better" has become the key word, we have seen a steady hike in the size of the Bichon in order to be able to compete in the Group. Also, when our Standard eliminated the wording of "slightly longer than tall" we began to hear our winning dogs praised for their shorter backs and higher on leg with great reach and drive. There was no mention of how well muscled they were, we have begun to see a poor Poodle type evolving.

Essential to the Bichon are legs well set under the body, a pronounced sternum, large round dark eyes, good pigment, correct tail set, and, above all, a merry disposition. And, of course, a size under twelve inches at the shoulder. Balance is everything.

At the present time the greatest challenge to the breed is the proliferation of those who see the breeding of Bichons as a means of getting rich quick. With its sculptured look now prevalent in the ring, the Bichon has become a handler's breed, who with their expertise with the scissors, and their fast movement around the ring, are able to camouflage serious faults.

I believe that the individual breed clubs should conduct seminars in which the standards of the Bichon and Poodle should be studied along with presenting a live Bichon and a white Poodle so that each person present would see the difference between the two breeds.

Pam Goldman
Camelot Bichons

Over the twenty plus years I've been in Bichons, there have been several dogs that were close to the Standard. I recall Ch. Ole' Rhondi, a nicely balanced, good moving dog with presence, perhaps a little ahead of his time in silhouette. There was Ch. Unicorns Nicholas Nickelbee. I liked his package, head and way of going. Ch. Tres Beau Decor was a small package of energy that had a beautiful head and attitude galore. His size and shape fit the Standard before we changed it in 1988. To my great regret, there were dogs I never saw, such as Ch. Vogelflight's Music Man and Ch. Chaminade Syncopation. Also, must not forget Ch. Devon Puff and Stuff, lovely outline, great personality in the ring. She did a lot for the breed.

Of course, in answer to which of my own dogs had the greatest influence, I must say Ch. Camelot's Brassy Nickel CDX. He made my childhood dream of having a Best in Show dog come true in a big way! Because of Nicky, recognition came my way and I became a judge of Bichon Frises. Most of what I know about good movement he taught me. Certainly, he showed me what makes a great show dog. At sixteen, he still has the carriage and attitude that made him a great winner.

In answer to your third question, I'd have to say "yes, we've sacrificed a lot for glamour!" We have a lot of pretty faces and coats with four legs that go nowhere. It's a disappointment to walk down a lineup of lively looking dogs and the to discover how unsound many of them are. Attention must be paid to four good legs, length of body and neck, tail carriage and especially temperament.

Essential to Bichon type is a proper head with muzzle to skull ratio of 3:5. Facial pigment and correct eye shape and placement are key, in my opinion. Tail set and carriage also contribute to proper balance and outline. Correct, easy flowing motion completes the picture.

I think that the greatest challenge facing the Bichon Frise today is the result of the practice of many of our well known, prominent breeders of requiring puppies back from every bitch sold. This leads to indiscriminate breeding and "instant experts" now "breeders" who have no idea of what the Standard really calls for, no conception of how to use a pedigree and no real breeding program. Co-ownership of every puppy sold, even pets, contributes to a serious problem. Not every puppy is a show or breeding prospect and breeders who really care about the breed must accept this fact and not be concerned about ROMs and ROMXs.

Those two designations have contributed much to the breed's problems, as people breed for quantity and forget about quality.

The solution? I'm not sure. Drop ROMs and ROMXs. Sell puppies to pet owners without making "breeders" and "exhibitors" out of them. Spay and neuter those puppies that are going to pet homes. We need to remember that QUALITY is more important than quantity.

Mary Ellen and Andrew ("Gene") Mills
Drewlaine Bichons

Our choice for the Bichon that most closely represented the standard would be the bitch, **Ch. Excell Balverne Joy Of Spring** bred and owned by Joy Bryant—a Specialty Best In Show, Group and all Breed Best in Show winner. I believe Joy had about as much in the type and soundness departments as any Bichon, dog or bitch, that has been shown. Her head and expression was everything you could ask for without being overdone. She was beautifully balanced and could stand on her own in the ring. She had a lovely temperament and could be relied upon to give her all every time she was shown.

Though not as charismatic as Joy the contribution of **Ch. Chaminade Mr. Beau Monde** can not be overlooked. He set type for the breed and were he to walk into our rings today could still earn his title with little or no problem.

Certainly we can not underestimate the influence of **Ch. Beau Monde the Huckster**. He proved to be particularly dominant in correct balance and proportion and in the profile movement so typical of the well made Bichon.

Ch. Cali-Col's Villanelle, our foundation bitch, not only produced champions, she contributed her producing ability to 6 consecutive generations of champion and champion producing bitches. She was able to pass on her balance and femininity to her daughters and yet was able to accept the qualities of the sires she was mated to as well. She was indeed a gold mine of producing ability.

If the breed has been affected negatively by "coat and glamor" it is because some breeders and judges simply can not see beyond the breed's coat. The standard clearly outlines the proportions our breed must have and makes no allowance for how well faults are disguised by clever trimming. I do not believe our coats are as much a problem as the inability of some individuals to learn what is beneath them.

There are few breeds more elegant and attractive than the well constructed and well balanced Bichon

Frise. I think not having been able to include the descriptive phrase ("There is something about a really stylish Bichon Frise in proportion and stance that reminds of a little show pony") in our standard was a real disservice to the breed. Those few words said much about character and balance—essentials in the quality Bichon.

The correct reach and drive found in the Bichon's profile movement is a hallmark of the breed. Tom Stevenson remarked on this in the early days of our breed and it stands to this day.

When the balance, proportion and movement are achieved there is nothing more pleasing than to have it appear behind the beautifully made Bichon head.

There is no question that the challenge we faced in the beginning is the same one we face now—short legs and long bodies—the drag of the breed. There is nothing in any of the breed standards from the original written in France in 1933 to ours in the present that indicate that we should relent in our struggle away from this fault. Should anyone doubt it is the drag of the breed they only need look at the dwarf types that come from the puppy mills and slip shod breeding programs of the world—invariably short of leg and long of body.

We must constantly, in seminars as well as in what we write, stress the importance of correct proportions and proper balance.

Judith Thayer
Jadele's Bichons

Closest to the standard? **Ch. Devon's Puff and Stuff**, because I think she displays the overall picture, beauty, balance and the proper temperament the breed should have.

The Bichon owned by me that was the most instrumental in helping me toward my goals was **Ch. Jadele's March Freddy**, the sire of nine AKC champions. Why? Because he was dominant for producing even, jaunty, showy temperaments with correct layback of shoulders, dark pigment, medium bone, substance, correct type, small to medium size and good movement.

I don't feel that the emphasis on coat and glamour in the modern Bichon has had any effect on conformation and movement.

The characteristics that are most essential to Bichon type are coat texture and correct temperament, proper structure, layback of shoulders, and angulation of the rear legs. They must be moderately balanced in body length with a well pronounced forechest. Correct tail carriage, a properly proportioned head and muzzle length with eyes that are round and forward looking combined with dark pigment, medium bone, scissors bite, straight front legs and round feet with thick pads complete the picture. The coat is trimmed with no exaggerations and is preferably all white in color.

I feel that the greatest challenge facing the breed today is to breed the Bichon to be moderately balanced and proportioned with the jaunty, happy attitude. We should deal with this challenge by breeding for good temperaments and for moderate balance, gradually breeding the correct leg length and not producing a dog too leggy nor too short in back, and by continually breeding this correct balance and good temperament for each generation.

Chapter VIII

INTERNATIONAL BREEDERS GALLERY

The following pages
contain noted Bichons
from across the United States as well as
Canada, Finland, Sweden, Brazil, Australia, New Zealand
and Japan.

The little white street dog from Europe has come
a very long way.

AVAGEE'S

Ch. AvaGee's Mississippi ShoBoat, BISS, ROM
Ch. Brereton Ricochet Romance X Brereton Miss of AvaGee's, ROM

"Skipper" was owner-handled to 121 Bests of Breed, 26 Group placements, 6 Group Firsts and a BISS. He was rated in the Top Ten in Breed and Group ratings in 1991. He was Veteran Dog at the BFCA National Specialty 1994. He is the sire of Ch. Kady J's Huckelberry Finn, BIS and Ch. Koblenz Miss Carol Ann, multiple Group winner.

He was our first home bred Champion and at eleven, he is still clown of the house. NT199736

George & Avanell Sikes
4 Chartres
Brandon, Mississippi 39042

BAUDIER, REG.

Ch. Baudier Vogelflight Dream

Ch. Petit Four Vogelflight Marco (10 Chs) X Woodway Wynne De Baudier (8 Chs & 2 others ptd.)

Dream's first points, BW for a 5 point major, from the American Bred class at the BFC of Greater Houston's first Specialty, judge nancy Shapland, in an entry of 15d, 29b and 2d, 3b Specials. Dream finished with 4, 3, 4 point majors, Bests of Breeds over Specials, and a Group placement from the classes. She has multiple Group placements and is Wynne's 3rd Champion with a Group II. Her litter sister, Magic, was Wynne's 8th Champion and is herself a Champion producer of 3 (one a multiple Group winner) with 4 others being shown.

Dream has had a very limited number of offspring, her son, Ch. Baudier's Dash N Dream Machine finishing makes Dream, Wynne's 9th Champion producer and the final of Wynne's 8 Chs to become a Ch. producer. Wynne's 9 Champion producers have produced a total of 29 Champions to date, others pointed, with several being shown, others yet to be shown. Dream is a smaller boned version of her dam, with her sire's expression. She was finished and co-owned by Mary & Kathy Vogel, Vogelflight.

OFA 43G/CERF 91/Patellar BCF-8A 1/62/F-T

Michael Husband
8125 River Drive
Houston, Texas 77017-3617 USA
713-242-9101

CHAMINADE

Ch. Chaminade Chamour Giovanni
Ch. Chaminade Chamour Jonathan
Ch. Chaminade Chamour Chances Ar
Ch. Chaminade Chamour Petrouska
...and Bill McFadden

CHAMINADE

Ch. Chaminade Chamour Chances Ar

We consider Ch. Chaminade Chamour Chances Ar (Ch. Alpenglow Ashley du Chamour x Ch. Chaminade Chamour Diva) to be an outstanding example of a long term goal to establish a dominant breed type. A breed and Group II winner at Westminster Kennel Club (1995) Chance proved this type is appreciated.

It began three decades ago with foundation Bichons Petit Galant, Ami du Kilkanny and Robspierre and progressed with Ch. Chaminade Tempo, whose influence was paramount.

The opposite page shows four Bichons; all have different sire and dams. The uniformity and quality are obvious. We are pleased to have established a line that is both correct and distinctive.

Barbara B. Stubbs
5769 Beaumont Avenue
La Jolla, CA 92037-7307
619-454-6984 Fax: 619-454-6756

CHAMOUR

Am. Can. Ch. Craigdale's Ole' Rhondi

It started with a call from Dale Hunter of Vancouver, Canada. A 10 month old puppy from the breeding of her Christopher daughter to my double Tempo grandson had been returned. After dematting, a bath, and scissoring, she thought he looked good but she couldn't keep a male. He would be sent to me, as show dog or pet. Price, $200.00 (remember, it was 1981). Within 24 hours after he arrived, I sent her a contract for 3 free stud services - this was no $200.00 dog. His head was the most beautiful I've ever seen, but his body and soundness were hard to beat and he has passed this on down to his get. Through his son, Beemer, and grandson, Ashley, and their get, they have accounted for 6 National Specialty Best of Breeds and 5 Westminster wins - 2 Group Firsts, 1 Group Second and 2 Group Thirds plus Ole' having a Group Three there himself.

Breeder: Dale Hunter   Owners: Lois Morrow & Barbara Stubbs

Lois Morrow
79-390 Fazio Lane South
La Quinta, CA 92253
760-564-0515 Fax: 760-771-0515

CHAMOUR

Ch. Alpenglow Ashley Du Chamour
Ch. Craigdale Saluto Du Chamour x Ch. Chaminade Blue Velvet

ASHLEY   1985 - 1993

We all have had certain dogs that come to mind as being the great showman, great sire, or great companion. Ashley was all the above in a beautiful 10 3/4" body. He was the smallest Bichon to do as much winning as he did - 12 BIS, 1 BFCA National Specialty and #1 Non Sporting dog in 1988. But what he did for our breeding program surpassed his win records. We lost him at the age of eight to pesticide sprayed by an exterminator but even with the limited breeding he sired over 20 champions. His strongest influence is showing up in his get when bred to the Beemer line. A son, Ch. Chaminade Chamour Chances Ar was Group Two at Westminster 1995 and a grandson, Ch. Craigdale Yoannewyn El Toro was Best of Breed at the 1996 National.

Breeders: Barbara Stubbs & Linda Daye

Lois Morrow
79-390 Fazio Lane South
La Quinta, CA 92253
760-564-0515 Fax: 760-771-0515

Owner: Lois Morrow

CHAMOUR

Am. Mex. Intl. Ch. Chaminade Le Blanc Chamour
Am.Can. Ch. Craigdale's Ole' Rhondi x Ch. Chamour's Finale

BEEMER 1987 -

Beemer came from a breeding planned to bring Tempo back in from the dam's side but the breeding almost went awry at whelping. Weighing in at less than 3 ounces, he was pushed aside as an afterbirth and almost left there. As a youngster he was very small, but sound and elegant...and then grew to be the largest in his litter. His show record was impressive: 13 Bests in Show, Best of Breed National Specialty 1989 and 1990, Group One 1990 and Group Three 1991 at Westminster, and as a Veteran, came back for an Award of Merit at the 1995 National Specialty. Beemer and his son "JP", the top winning male Bichon, now make a lovely duo, whether curled up on the bed asleep or out at the end of their leads when going for a walk - as though they were in for BIS at Westminster again.

Breeders:
Lois Morrow
Barbara Stubbs
George & Nancy Harrell

**Lois Morrow
79-390 Fazio Lane South
La Quinta, CA 92253
760-564-0515 Fax: 760-771-0515**

Owners:
Lois Morrow
Carolyn & Richard Vida

CHAMOUR

Ch. Chaminade Larkshire Lafitte
Ch. Chaminade Le Blanc Chamour x Ch. Chaminade Hollyhock Heather

JP   1990 -

JP, whose sire, grandsire, and great grandsire have accounted for a Group One, 2 Group Threes and a Group Four at Westminster, seemed destined to accomplish great things there too. Just 18 months old, out one month as a Special, he went to Westminster and won the breed, the following year a Group One, the next, a Group Three. A beautifully put together dog, elegant, very sound front and rear with an exceptional attitude in the ring. One look says "this is a male." JP was the first Bichon Bill McFadden handled, but with his great eye for a dog he quickly excelled in trimming and brought out the best in temperament. The "Bill and JP mutual admiration society" achieved #1 male Bichon ever, 47 Bests in Show, over 200 Group Firsts, 13 Specialties including two BFCA Nationals and in the Top Ten dogs all breed in 1993 and 1994.

Breeders:
Lois Morrow
Barbara Stubbs
Linda Rowe

Lois Morrow
79-390 Fazio Lane South
La Quinta, CA 92253
760-564-0515 Fax: 760-771-0515

Owners:
Lois Morrow

CHAMOUR

Am. Can. Ch. Craigdale Yoannewyn El Toro
Yoannewyn's Cap't Barnstaple x Ch. Kibbatts Craigdale Joy
TORO   1992 -

Toro's pedigree is an example of a total outcross that worked, not just in Toro himself, but his ability as a stud dog. Whether linebred or outcrossed, his get are coming up with his elegance, lovely head, easy reach and drive and tremendous coat. His sire, Yoannewyn's Cap't Barnstaple, is from the great English line "Sulyka". The dam, Ch. Kibbats Craigdale Joy, had Ashley as a sire and Beemer's litter sister as her dam. This litter sister was BOS to Beemer at the 1989 National Specialty. Toro was Specialed for only one year and had 3 Bests in Show and was Best of Breed at the 1996 National Specialty under breeder judge, Ann Hearn. Toro has now returned to Canada to live with Dick and Pat McCallister who took him through puppyhood and finished his Canadian & American championships.

Breeder:
Patricia Dale Hunter

Lois Morrow
79-390 Fazio Lane South
La Quinta, CA 92253
760-564-0515 Fax: 760-771-0515

Owners:
Dick & Pat McCallister
2122 Corvis Rd, RR 1, Sooke
Canada V0S 1N0
250-642-2310

DEVON

Ch. Devon Puff And Stuff
April 28, 1982 - August 9, 1995

Puff is the top winning Bichon Frise in the history of the breed. Her record includes 276 Bests of Breed; 167 Group Firsts, and 60 Bests in Show; Show Dog of the Year - Kennel Review Tournament of Champions and Purina Invitational; Kennel Ration Show Dog of the Year for Non-Sporting Group; Back to back Group Firsts at Westminster; and two consecutive National Specialties. She was a breeder's dream and is greatly missed. Puff produced one litter, and is the dam of 3 Champions.

Bred, owned and loved by:
Nancy Shapland
Three Greencroft Drive
Champaign, IL 61821
E-Mail: Bilmel8ter@ AOL.com

DIAMANT

BISS/BIS Ch. Diamant's Le Magnifique ROMX

Since 1983 Diamant has bred quality Bichon Frises, with an emphasis on soundness and breed type, for a total of 24 champions. Pictured above is our top winner and producer, BISS/BIS Ch. Diamant's Le Magnifique ROMX. "Dex" did exceptionally well in the show ring. He finished undefeated with 5 majors and a Group 1. As a Special he won a BISS, 2 BIS, 42 Group Firsts and 120 BOB awards. "Dex" has also excelled as a producer, with 30 champion offspring. **FIVE** of these are BIS or BISS winners which gives him the all time record for the most BIS/BISS offspring.

Not only does "Dex" have top producers behind him; a great grandfather and grandfather with 38 and 36 champions, and mother and father with 9 and 11 champions; he has sired producers, three of which have already produced more than 10 champions each.

It is satisfying to know that the Diamant bloodline is in many fine pedigrees and that the quality is continuing.

CERF: BCF 589/95-111, OFA: BCF 342G36M

Kay Hughes
2371 Live Oak Drive East
Los Angeles, CA 90068 USA
213-461-7190

DIAMELLA

Finnish & Swedish Ch. Diamella Toy Soldier

This outstanding youngster is one of Diamella's several champions. He is an example of the quality, type and size that I have always wanted and tried to breed. He won for example BEST OF BREED at the show where there was the largest entry of Bichon Frises (as of this date) in Finland. This boy made a record and won over 89 Bichon Frises under judge, Mr. August De Wilde from Belgium.

The Finnish Kennel Club has admitted the very valued VUOLASVIRTA prize to Diamella Kennel for breeding top quality Bichon Frises in Finland.

Jaana M. Karenmaa
Pyharannantie 270
26950 VOILUOTO
FINLAND
Tel: 358-2-8211394
E-mail: http://jaana.karenmaa@usa.net

DREWLAINE

Ch. Drewlaine Beau Monde Batiste

Ch. Devon Viva Poncho (Ch. Tomaura's Moonlight Sonata ex Ch. C & D's Devon Hell's Lil' Angel)
ex
Ch. Drewlaine's Beau Monde Deja Vu (Ch. Beau Monde The Huckster ex Ch. Drewlaine's Eau de Love)

Batiste made her ring debut by winning Reserve Winners Bitch at the BFCA 1987 Specialty under Frank Sabella. Shown by Michael Kemp, she went on to finish her championship in short order. Shown sparingly as a Special she was a consistent Best of Breed winner with a number of Group placements as well. Whelped March 9, 1986. Breeders: Mr. & Mrs. A.G. Mills & Richard Beauchamp.

Drewlaine - Quality

Mr. & Mrs. A.G. Mills	Richard Beauchamp	Nancy Shapland
3870 Avenue San Miguel	1071 Main Street #4	3 Greencroft
Bonita, CA 92002	Cambria, CA 93428	Champaign, IL 61821

DREWLAINE

Ch. Beau Monde Drewlaine Durango

Ch. Beau Monde Top Banana (Ch. Sumarco Alaafee Top Gun ex Ch. Dibett Cameo Rose Drewlaine)
ex
Ch. Drewlaine Beau Monde Batiste (Ch. Devon Viva Poncho ex Ch. Drewlaine's Beau Monde Deja Vu)

Durango - Type, soundness, style and quality. Another outstanding group winner from the fifth generation of the Drewlaine-Beau Monde bloodlines. His proportions, quality and elegance are being passed on to his offspring. Whelped May 16, 1991. Breeders: Mr. & Mrs. A.G. Mills, Richard Beauchamp and Nancy Shapland.

through the years

Cecelia Ruggles & Lori Kornfield
129 Eleven Levels Road
Ridgefield, CT 06877
(203) 438-5558

DREAMS CAME TRUE

Am.Ch., Br.Gr.Ch., Int.Ch., PamAm Ch., Arg.Ch., Parag.Ch., Americas & Caribean Ch.
Ch. Dreams Came True's The Phantom
Br. Great National Winner

In 1984, while attending a dog show, we fell in love with the Bichon Frise. Our first puppies, *S.E. Reve d'Amour* - **"Jolie"** - and *Etoile do Aruan* - **"Tuka"**, were the first Bichon bitches to receive International & South American Championships. In 1992, through our friend Sonia Ehllermann, we purchased *Avana Mickey Mouse of Sulyka* from Sue Dunger, in England. **"Mickey"** finished in 1993 as the #1 Bichon, #1 Non Sporting and #5 All Breed Dog in Brazil. He has also made a great impact on our breeding program as he is the sire of all 5 of our American Champions. We were having great success in our country, but a phone call in 1993 to the US to Barbara Stubbs (Chaminade) and Mimi Winkler (Judges Choice), would broaden our success enormously. Barbara, our dear *"Godmother"*, introduced us to the *American Bichon Family*. In February 1995, we brought *Dreams Came True's Jennifer* to Mimi. That May, at the BFCA National Specialty, **"Jenny"** won Best Puppy in Sweeps and two months later we had our first American Champion. In August 1995, we sent to Mimi our special "**Gasparzinho**" (pictured here), who finished his championship in 5 shows and won, in 1997, BOS at the Pier (NY) Specialty. In February '96, we also brought to Mimi *Dreams Came True Triumph* - **"Paco"**, who won, that May, BOS Puppy Sweeps, from the 6-9 months class, at the BFCA National Specialty. **"Paco"** is now the #2 Bichon, with over 20 all breed BIS and is the #3 Non Sporting Dog, that made us the #16 breeders in US. We are equally proud of our other American Champions: *Dreams Came True Jordy* who finished in the Top 20 in 1997 and *Dreams Came True's Oliver*, the Best Puppy at the World Dog Show in Belgium, in 1995. Many people have dreams, but we are very lucky ones, because our **DREAMS CAME TRUE**!

Cristina & Roberto da Veiga
Phone/fax: 55-11-493-7579   E-mail: roberto.veiga@netcomp.com.br
Sao Paulo, Brazil

EVIVAS
BICHONS & POODLES

Int & Fin & Est Ch. Evivas Royal-Q-Diana
Est W-94, PZ JW - 93

Sarabande Silver Mink	Primo's Tugg D'War
Petite Ami's Fady Boy	Sassas Super Short
Crubow's Nolen Volen	Jara's Super Sassa
Sired by: **Int & Fin & S & Lux & Est Ch. Sangres Quick Quiller**	Out of: **Int & SF & DK MVA Ch. Azurs Orchid**
Violar Exellent-Raphsodi	Azurs Lordjim
Petite Ami's Ebba at Sangre	Azurs Royal Rosebutton
Tsingfu's Mad Louise	Azurs Maiden

Home of 67 Champions & 17 International Champions

Eva & Ivar Hedman
Kelotie 1
Fin-04260 Kerava, Finland
Tel. & Fax: Int+358+ (0) 9 244 599

FOUNTAINBLEU

Ch. Fountainbleu Peek A Boo ICU

This beautiful bitch is pictured taking a Best of Breed over Specials and later that day she took a Group II. She has a great personality along with a pretty face, plush coat and jet black pigment.

Fountainbleu dogs are loved before everything else - and then shown in breed conformation - and then in the obedience ring.

Mrs. Toby B. Frisch
Mrs. Andrea Frisch-Barbakoff
P.O. Box 35
Lake Grove, NY 11755 USA
516-467-7510
e-mail: tbfrisch@juno.com

GAYLOR

A "Type"ical Gaylor Threesome!

Pictured (center) with two of his champion get is Ch. Gaylors Mr. Magic of Glenelfred who finished his championship at eleven months of age with a five point major at the Southern New England Specialty. He went on to be a top winning Special three consecutive years...and was BFCA Sire of the Year in 1994. Magic is a solid producing sire that had 3 of his get in the Top Ten in the same year. Thanks to Magic and our foundation bitch, Ch. Gaylor's Krystal Princess, we have produced generations of soundness, lovely thick coats, black pigment and wonderful temperaments.

We are proud of our record here at Gaylor and are looking forward toward the future generations of champions. Among Magic's champion offspring are: BIS, BISS Ch. Goldcoast Saks Jackpot, BISS Ch. Gaylors Wizard of Mischief, Ch. Gaylors Goldcoast Obsession, Ch. Gaylors Hocus Pocus and Ch. Glenelfred U Lite Up My Life.

Gail Antetmoaso   Laurie Scarpa   Krista Fileccia
1 Dolphin Drive
Massapeque, New York 11758 USA
(516) 799-6871
Fax: (516) 799-1032

INGHEDENS KENNEL

One of our breeding groups (all dogs bred by the same breeder)

Photo by Harry Sirvo

20 years with Bichons in Sweden

INGER ADEHEIMER
Svanvagen 21
S-139 41 Varmdo
Sweden
Phone: 46 8 571 412 55
Fax: 46 8 571 409 05
e-mail: Lars@healthmedia.se

LARS ADEHEIMER

Approved F.C.I. judge
for over 100 breeds in
Terriers, Sighthounds
Toys, Utility
and other groups.

JUDGES CHOICE

Ch. Judges Choice Diamond Jim

In a relatively short breeding program, Judges Choice has produced over twenty-five champions. Ch. Judges Choice Purple Rain was my first homebred champion - she produced BISS Ch. Judges Choice B'way Bruiser and the 1995 Winners Bitch at the BFCA National Specialty, Ch. Judges Choice Divine Ms. M's. In 1997, Ch. Judges Choice Diamond Jim, at the tender age of thirteen months, was the Winners Dog at the BCFA National Specialty. He has since won many breeds and group placements and finished in the top twenty Bichons for 1997.

I am very excited about my breeding program as I am combining the best lines of the United States, England and Brazil. Is this "As Good As It Gets"? The best is yet to come!

Mimi Winkler
1 Aurora Lane
New Rochelle, NY 10804
(914) 235-9339

JOLINE

Sunny
CH. C & D'S SUNBEAM

Winkie
CH. KEYSTONE CHRISTINE

Blizzard
CH. C & D'S BEAU MONDE BLIZZARD

Banjo
CH. VOGELFLIGHT'S MUSICMAN

Huck
CH. BEAU MONDE'S THE HUCKSTER

Crystal
CH. CROCKERLY BEAU MONDE ECLIPSE

Rhondi
CH. D'SHAR'S RENDEZVOUS DU CHAMOR

Ole
CH. CRAIGDALE'S OLE RHONDI

Tuck
CH. TRES JOLIE MR. VAGABOND

Dex
CH. DIAMANT'S LE MAGNIFIQUE

Beemer
CH. CHAMINADE LE BLANC CHAMOUR

Skids
CH. BEAU MONDE TOP BANANA

Shilo
CH. JOLINE'S SHILO

Beau
CH. SEASTAR'S BEAU BRUMMEL

Beepers
CH. SEASTAR'S IN A HEARTBEAT

Donny
CH. SEASTAR'S DON JUAN

Tulips
CH. VOGELFLIGHT'S BAUDIER TULIP

Paco
CH. DREAMS CAME TRUE'S TRIUMPH

...plus many, many champions

Ch. Joline's Shilo

From Ch. Chaminade Mr. Beau Monde in the Miscellaneous class in 1972 to now...it's been a great journey. Thanks to Richard Beauchamp and Barbara Stubbs, we have had the privilege of exhibiting, owning and breeding some of the most influential dogs in this breed whose impact on the Bichon Frise will continue forever - all over the world.

The list above contains the still top sire of the breed and two others in the top five, the mother of the second top producing dam in the breed, the first Best in Show bitch, the first male to win a National Specialty, the first female to win a National Specialty, a Westminster Group winner and a two time Quaker Oats winner, plus many Specialties and Bests in Show.

Handlers:

Breeders-owners:
Pauline & Joseph Waterman
14100 Oakdale Drive
Lake Matthews, Perris, CA 92570
(909) 789-0635

"PACO"

Ch. Dreams Came True's Triumph
Ch. Avana Mouse Of Sulyka x Heaven Sent To Me DeNainarann

A wonderful cheerful, affectionate dog with immense breed type.
He fits the breed standard - planes, inches, balance and proportion are all there.
His first year of campaign has garnered him more Groups and Bests in Show than any other, so far.

Breeders:	Owners:	Handler:
Cristina & Roberto Veiga	**Nan Eisley Bennett**	(909) 789-0635
Brazil	**Susan C. McMillan**	Joe Waterman
	Mimi Winkler	
	Jill Cohen	

MARQUISE

Ch. Cabochon Batmadison Marquise
Ch. Yoannewyn's Hela Va Scorcher X Craigdale Espana

With our first Bichon Frise, CH. Diamant Jungle Gardenia ("Sheena"), Marquise was established in the early 1990's. From her first litter came our first homebred champion, CH. Marquise Chenin Blanc. "Cheni's" show career began with a Best in Match win, at our first A-Match under judge, Richard Beauchamp.

"Madison", pictured above at eight months, brought new fame to Marquise in 1997. His first win at seven months, Best in Sweepstakes, BFCNC Specialty was followed by Best in Sweepstakes BFCA National Specialty and Best in Sweepstakes BFCC (Canada) National Specialty.

There are many individuals who helped Marquise achieve success. Those who deserve special thanks and recognition are Kay Hughes (Diamant), W. Anne Yocom (Yoannewyn) and Pat McAllister (Cabochon).

As a current member of several dog organizations, and most actively The Bichon Frise Club of Greater Los Angeles, Marquise is committed to the betterment of the Bichon Frise.

**Sandra J. Madia
13631 Addison Street
Sherman Oaks, California 91436-1411
Ph: 818-784-4240 Fax: 818-784-5753
e-mail: marquise@westworld.com**

NORMANDY

Can.Am.Ch. Tondia's Brite Eyes-Bushy Tail, ROM

"Bites" (as he is lovingly known) is Normandy Bichons' foundation stud. He is a double "Music Man" grandson, bred by Nan and Burton Busk of California. "Bites" is well-known in Canada, as he has been featured on the cover of The Canadian Kennel Club Book of Dogs since 1988. Over the years we have bred selectively, and carefully introduced new lines with a view to producing Bichons of excellent quality, health, and temperament, and we have been well rewarded. We have bred many Canadian Champions under the Normandy prefix, as well as some American Champions; received Pedigree Breeder of the Year Awards in 1991 and 1993; and our Bichons have graced the covers of two prominent Canadian publications. The genetic influence of "Bites" is evident in our Normandy lines and will have a lasting effect on future generations of Bichons. Visit our Website at http://members.tripod.com/~Normandy/bichon.htm

Norma J. & Bill Dirszowsky
12 Mill Pond Lane
Udora, Ontario, Canada L0C 1L0
Telephone or Fax: 705-228-1148
e-mail: Normandy@BichonFrise.com

NUAGE

Ch. Nuage Hot Scandal

Scandal finished by going Best of Winners at the Greater New York Bichon Frise Club Specialty. I am very fortunate to have started with what I refer to as the best of the best. My first Bichon, Ch. Alpenglow Facsimile Chamour (a repeat of "Ashley") has won an Award of Merit at both the BFCA National Specialty as well as The Westminster Kennel Club. He most recently won the Veteran Dog Class at the BFCA National Specialty.

My second Bichon, Ch. Joline's The White Minx has an impressive pedigree with four of six dogs in the first two generations multiple BIS and BISS winners. "Minx" has proved to be a quality producer and was Dam of the Year, 1997, for a 5 champion litter. Her 7 Champion get to date include Ch. Nuage Hot Scandal, Ch. Nuage Summer Snow, Ch. Nuage Chamour Dilettante Val, Ch. Nuage Amazing Alexis (Alexis was Best Puppy In Show at the 1996 BFCA National Specialty), Ch. Nuage Chloe Narcisse, Ch. Joline's Frosting of Nuage, and Ch. Nuage Jaime Pheef La Petite.

Bill Dreker
Los Angeles, California
310-479-8654

PINEFIELD
EST 1977

Australian Ch. Pinefield Sweet Revenge

A small kennel that has concentrated on soundness and pigment with true Bichon make and shape. Certified testing now standard.

John & Christine Kellow
"Pinefields"
Lot 12 Hemry Road
Little Hampton, South Australia 5250
Phone 61 8 8391 0681 Fax: 61 8 8231 3667

PAW MARK

Ch. Jalwin Just A Jiffy
1978 - 1994

OFA & CERF clear at 15 years

Jiffy was our first Bichon. With him as our foundation, we have produced some 57 champions at Paw Mark.

Jiffy has a wonderful pedigree that includes five top producers. He himself is a top producer with 22 champion offspring. He is the sire of multiple BIS winning Ch. Paw Mark's Talk of the Town, ROMX, Number 1 Bichon in 1984, and the sire of 1983 National Sweepstakes winner, Ch. Paw Mark's Pebbles of Brereton.

Jiffy is one of two top producers to win the National Specialty. He also has 7 All Breed Bests in Show and 36 Group Ones. Jiffy was bred by Ann D. Hearn.

Pauline Schultz
5502 Pelham Road
Durham, NC 27713
919-361-2253

PAW MARK

Ch. Paw Mark's Talk of the Town, ROMX
1981 - 1996

OFA & CERF clear at 13 1/2 years

Gabby is the top winning breeder-owner-handled Bichon in breed history. In 1984 he was Number 1 Bichon, Number 2 Non-Sporting Dog with 9 Bests in Show, 35 Group Firsts and 52 Group placements.

Gabby has an impressive pedigree that contains four top producing sires and two top producing dams.

Gabby has produced 25 champion children.

Pauline Schultz
5502 Pelham Road
Durham, NC 27713
919-361-2253

PAW MARK

Ch. Paw Mark PCon Everybody Duck

OFA & CERF clear

Quackers is a lovely dog that finished his championship from the puppy class and has several group placements.

More than a show dog, we expect greatness from him as a producer. His second litter produced a Best in Show dog, Ch. Paw Mark's Fire and Ice.

Breeders-Owners
Pauline Schultz, Paula Ryan, Ramona Lower, Connie Armitage
5502 Pelham Road
Durham, NC 27713
919-361-2253

PAW MARK

Ch. Paw Mark's Fire and Ice

OFA & CERF clear

Flame is a spectacular dog, finishing his championship at 8 1/2 months and winning Best of Breed from the puppy class at the Astro Dome. Flame is a multiple BIS and multiple Specialty winner. He was bred by Pauline Schultz, Paula Ryan, Ramona Lower & Connie Armitage. A daughter from his second litter was Best in Sweepstakes at the 1996 National Specialty.

We expect wonderful things from him as he matures.

Owners
Pauline Schultz & Cecelia Ruggles
5502 Pelham Road
Durham, NC 27713
919-361-2253

SAKS

Ch. Saks First Edition

Here at Saks Bichons we strive for quality and elegance in our breeding program. Our commitment is to breed Bichons outstanding in breed type and soundness of movement. Our foundation Bichons are from the Sandcastle and Goldcoast lines.

"Pia" (pictured) is the latest result of our breeding program, finishing at 11 months of age with three 4-point majors from the puppy class and a major from the Bred By class. She is the daughter of Am/Can Ch. Goldcoast Saks Jackpot ("Kash") the 1995 Best of Breed National Specialty winner (3 BIS, 2 BISS) and Ch. Saks Susses Bezay ("Bizzi") Best Opposite Sex at the 1995 National Specialty and multiple Group placements. Pia, a double up on Ch. Sandcastle Bikini and Ch. Sandcastle Goldcoast Dixie, truly embodies elegance, type and beautiful movement.

Sandra & Kieth Hanson
6225 Willow Drive
Hamel, Minnesota 55340
612-478-2974

RIME

Ch. Mizar Night Dancer of Rime

Since 1982 I have enjoyed sharing my life with my Bichon Frise companions. My orientation has been to proceed slowly and selectively; intending to faithfully carry forward the endeavors of the many breeders whose achievements I gratefully enjoy.

Mizar (by Ch. C and D's King of the Road out of C and D's Xmas Maid aka Riff) embodies the classic beginnings from which Rime Bichons have evolved. He was the first shown and finished from our foundation, Riff, and he remains important in today's pedigrees.

Deborah Wentz
Post Office Box 3602
Ann Arbor, Michigan 48106
Phone: 734-761-2111 Fax: 734-761-9383

RIME

Rime Call Me Mr. Blue

Collaborating with serious fanciers has been a pleasure and productive: my Bichons have been blessed with outstanding intelligence, temperament, and expression as well as soundness, solid drive, good reach and flowing movement.

Mr. Blue (by Ch. Dove-Cotes Hakuna Matata out of Rime A Stitch In Time) is pictured at nine months. He represents our dogs today and with his litter sister, Ch. Rime Finally Fifine, will carry us handsomely into the future.

The Future

Deborah Wentz
Post Office Box 3602
Ann Arbor, Michigan 48106
Phone: 734-761-2111 Fax: 734-761-9383

RIME

Ch. Rime Finally Fifine

Fifine's career got off the ground with her win of the 12 to 18 month class at the National Specialty judged by Anne Rogers Clark in 1997. She finished quickly in the Fall of that year,

. . . is NOW!

Deborah Wentz
Post Office Box 3602
Ann Arbor, Michigan 48106
Phone: 734-761-2111 Fax: 734-761-9383

SHANDAU

New Zealand Ch. Shandau Eager Beaver

Bred for correct type pigment and movement

**Shandau Kennels
Elsie Rennie
Horseshoe Bush Road, Dairy Flat, RD 4 Albany
Auckland, New Zealand
Telephone & fax: 0942-63845**

SPECIAL TIMES

Ch. Special Times Slam Dunk

Pictured is one of our young homebred champions, Ch. Special Times Slam Dunk.
In just five years of showing Bichons and just three of breeding, we seem able to accomplish a lot but, believe, the most
Special of the Times
are still to come!

Commited to True Bichon Frise Type.

Eleanor McDonald
52 Garden Road
Scarsdale, NY 10583
(914) 723-4714
Fax: (914) 723-4605

TEJADA

Australian Champion Tejada Revenge From Hell

Revenge is now residing in Japan with his new owners, the famous FRAU SCHLOSS Kennels. Before he left Australia, he was a multi Group and In Show winner and produced some magnificent progeny. Now in Japan, he has already produced a Best in Show All Breeds winner. He, with the Tejada bitches in Japan, will make a great contribution to the breed there.

Keiko Mizuno & Michiko Enokida
816 Hanasaki-cho
Narita-Shi Chiba Ken
Japan
Phone-Fax: 81-476-938978

TEJADA

Australian Champion
Tejada Charisma Ova Hell

the bitch
Tejada Whatsa Name

American & Australian Champion
Beau Monde Drewlaine Dry Ice (Imp USA)

Tejada is a small, quality kennel of world renown. Always the winner under breed specialist judges from the four continents Australia - United States of America - United Kingdom and Scandinavia.

Always striving for excellence.

Gerry Greig
12 Malva Road, Ferntree Gully
3156 Victoria, Australia
Phone 61-3-97582273
Fax: 61-3-97535580

VOGELFLIGHT
Multiple BIS, BISS since 1970

Ch. Vogelflight Baudier Tulip
Ch. Chez Sharri Ashton Vogelflight x Ch. Baudier Vogelflight Magic

Tulip's father "Ashton" is a very beautiful reflection of his sire: Alpenglow Ashley Chamour and she in turn a very feminine version of both her father and grandfather.

Measuring at 10 1/2 inches you can see her many beautiful qualities. Within her show career she has won multiple BISS and numerous group wins. Tulip had the distinction of going Best of Opposite Sex at Westminster in 1996 and Vogelflight Banana Puddin was also Best Opposite Sex at the 1997 Westminster the following year.

Vogelflight
Mary M. and Kathie D. Vogel
2400 London Bridge Road
Virginia Beach, VA 23456

WINDSTAR

Ch. Windstar's Mr. BoJangles

BJ - shown on a limited basis due to client obligations, finished his championship from the Bred by class, in grand style by winning breeds and group placements along the way. A pedigree worth its weight in gold comes from the breed's top producers on both sides of the pedigree, such as Ch. Vogelflight's Music Man (the breed's only three time National Specialty winner) and Ch. Chaminade Mr. Beau Monde (the breed's top producer). Not yet two and a half, BJ shows great promise for a wonderful future.

Twenty-seven years of dedicated breeding at Windstar has us producing pigment and temperaments which are stable and outstanding and those "pretty to die for" faces that have always been prevelant along with everything that makes a Bichon a Bichon.

Breeder/owner
Wendy and Estelle Kellerman
683 Bedford Avenue
Hauppauge, New York 11788 USA
(516) 361-2949   (718) 343-3336
email: WKBichon@aol.com.

ZIPADEDODA

Whelped March 3, 1992

Ch. Zipadedoda Hidden Meaning
There is almost nothing this extraordinary Bichon has not achieved.

Outright winner 1994 Australasian Dog of the Year (All Breeds) Competition ("ND/Friskies") - historic first for the Bichon and toy breeds in this country. Winner, to date, of 33 Bests in Show (including the 1993 Spring Fair - largest All Breeds Championship Show held by the RNSW Canine Council & including multi BISS), Royal Best in Group winner and sire of Royal & Spring Fair BOB winners.

Sired by NZ Ch. Kynismar Hidden Destiny (imp. UK) out of Ch. Zipadedoda Krisy Kringle

Zipadedoda is also the home of Ch. Kynismar Show Me Heaven (imp. UK) - "Aaron", son of Eng.Ch. Kynismar Heaven Sent to Roushka (England's all time top-winning homebred Bichon), litter brother of Eng.Ch. Kynismar Cherished Heaven (Top Bichon 1992 & 1993) and sire of Eng.Ch. Kynismar Feels Like Heaven (Top Bichon 1995). Bred by Myra Atkins, UK.

Julia Jeffrey
206 Annangrove Road, Annangrove, 2156
NSW, Australia
Telephone & Fax: 61 2 9679 0015

ZIPADEDODA

Ch. Zipadedoda Hidden Meaning's winning offspring

Ch. Zettamay Special Meaning, "Chance", DCC & BOB 1996 Sydney Royal at 14 months of age under Mrs. Michelle Billings, USA; BOB and Best in Group under Dr. Sam Draper, USA, at the 1996 Ku-Ring-Gai Autumn Carnival.
Aust & NZ Ch. Zipadedoda Miss D Mena, "Dee Dee", BCC & Runner-up BOB 1996 Sydney Royal at 12 months of age under Mrs. Billings. BOB and Best in Show, January '97, Otago Toy Championship Show, NZ, under Swedish breed specialist Lars Adeheimer with Ch. Zipadedoda Double Heaven, "Simon" (owned by Joanne Warman, NZ), DCC, Runner-up BOB and Runner-up in Show. Dee Dee is an "Aaron" granddaughter and Simon is his son. Chance and Dee Dee are pictured above (left and right).
Ch. Zipadedoda Lady Jane, Best Bitch Puppy in Breed under Mrs. Billings and Best of Breed at the 1996 Spring Fair.

All these winning "Meaning" offspring have different dams.

Zipadedoda - four generations of Best in Show & Sydney Royal Best of Breed winners.

Julia Jeffrey
206 Annangrove Road, Annangrove, 2156
NSW, Australia
Telephone & Fax: 61 2 9679 0015

WINWARD

Ch. Winward's Friendly Shadow
Ch. Sandon's Winter Shadow x Ch. Bonnie Colleen of Atlantis

Chris Henkel and Mary Ann Larssen are very proud to have produced their first homebred champion, "Dakota" after only eight years of showing dogs. They have finished four Bichons with Dakota being the first to carry their Winward kennel name. Dakota finished his championship at 12 months of age, handled by Martin Lavander. Briefly shown by George Temmel, longtime Bichon breeder. Dakota's career as a "special" began in earnest in July, 1997 when James Gerarge and his expert groomer, Kamiko Ono took over. At their first two shows, they won back to back Group 1's followed by a long string of breed wins and group placements. Not yet three years of age, Dakota, in January 1998, received Awards of Merit at Westminster and the New York and New Jersey specialties. He has been in the Top Ten Bichon Frise rankings since he started with Jim Gerarge.

Chris Henkel & Mary Ann Larssen
11225 Rabun Gap Drive
North Fort Myers, FL 33917-4224
(941) 567-0375
e-mail: Timberbend@AOL.com

Ch. Devon Puff and Stuff
Photographed by John Ashbey.

BIBLIOGRAPHY

Beauchamp, Richard G., *The Bichon Frise Handbook*, Rohman Publications, Hollywood Hills, California, 1972.

Beauchamp, Richard G., *The Bichon Frise Workbook*, Rohman Publications, North Hollywood, California, 1975.

Beauchamp, Richard G. *The Bichon Frise Today*, Rohman Publications, Los Angeles, California, 1982

Beauchamp, Richard G. Bichon Frise, *A Complete Pet Owner's Manual*, Barron's Educational Series, Inc., Hauppauge, New York, 1966.

Bichon Frise Club of America, Inc., *Illustrated Discussion of the Bichon Frise Standard*, Bichon Frise Club of America, Inc., 1988.

Bichon Frise Club of New South Wales, *A Decade of Bichons in Australia*, Bichon Frise Club of New South Wales, Sydney, Australia, 1986.

Brearly, J.M. & Nicholas, A.K., *This is the Bichon Frise*, T.F.H. Publications, Inc., Neptune City, New Jersey, 1973.

Fyfe, Jean, *Your Bichon Frise*, Joanne Anderson Publications, Auckland, New Zealand, 1988.

Hutchison, John E., *The Bichon Frise*, A Practical Approach, Jon Hutchison, Melbourne, Australia, 1986.

Mills, Mary Ellen & Andrew, *A New Owner's Guide to Bichon Frises*, T.F.H. Publications, Inc., Neptune City, New Jersey, 1977.

Ransome, Jackie, *The Dog Directory Guide to The Bichon Frise*, Dog Directory Publications, Bracknell, Berkshire, England, 1978.

Ransom, E. Jackie, *The Bichon Frise*, H.F. & G. Witherby, Ltd., London, England, 1988.

Stubbs, Barbara, *The Complete Bichon Frise*, Howell Book House, New York, New York, 1990.

SUGGESTED WEBSITES

Cyberpet: The Ultimate in Pet Information on the Web
http://www.cyberpet.com

Cyberpet is a huge source for finding Breeders, Breed information, Rescue contacts, training advice, pet products and more. Centralizing much of the internet's Pet information into one easy to use site, Cyberpet has won many top internet awards. Also available is the popular Cyberpet-Chat, posting boards, and invaluable articles geared toward both the pet owner and the experienced breeder. Cyberpet invites you to surf on by...

Top Dog Endeavors: Global Advertising at Hometown Prices
http://www.tdog.com

Founded in June 1997 Top Dog is visited over 50,000 times monthly and has been viewed by people in every American state, Canadian province and continent in the world. When you advertise with Top Dog you are also advertising in well known national publications such as Dog World, Dog Fancy, Dog Sports and the Match Show Bulletin as well as newspapers nationwide. Call or email for details on including your dogs or dog items: Tel: 410-439-3170; Fax: 410-439-3171; Email: info@tdog.com